THOMAS A. EDISON
And His
KINETOGRAPHIC
MOTION
PICTURES

THOMAS A. EDISON
AND HIS
KINETOGRAPHIC
MOTION PICTURES

By Charles Musser

PUBLISHED FOR THE
FRIENDS OF EDISON NATIONAL HISTORIC SITE
BY RUTGERS UNIVERSITY PRESS
NEW BRUNSWICK, NEW JERSEY

Thomas A. Edison and His Kinetographic Motion Pictures
by Charles Musser
p. cm.
ISBN 0-8135-2210-2
1. Kinetograph. 2. Kinetoscope. 3. Kineto-phonograph.
4. Motion pictures--United States--History.
5. Edison, Thomas A. (Thomas Alva), 1847-1931.
I. Title: Thomas A. Edison and his kintetographic motion pictures
TR885.M8   1993 93-96 CIP
778.5'34--dc20

Printed in the United States
First U.S. Edition
1 2 3 4 5 6 7 8 9 10

This publication was made possible in part
through a grant from the New Jersey Historical Commission.

Book design by Nina Ovryn
Cover photograph hand tinted by Elizabeth Lennard

ON THE TITLE PAGE:
A man viewing a peephole kintetophone and wearing
hearing tubes for accompanying sound, 1895.
Edison experimented with sound film from the start, but never
achieved synchronized sound and picture.

❧ CONTENTS ❧

Foreword

"I AM
EXPERIMENTING
UPON AN
INSTRUMENT
WHICH DOES FOR
THE EYE WHAT
THE PHONOGRAPH
DOES FOR
THE EAR, WHICH IS
THE RECORDING
AND REPRODUCTION
OF THINGS
IN MOTION. . ."

So wrote Thomas Edison in 1888. It was at Edison's West Orange laboratory that the first motion pictures were made, flickering strips of film that would form the basis of an enormous entertainment industry. Edison's role in the birth of motion pictures has long been the subject of lively debate; his earliest biographers gave all the honor to him, portraying the "Wizard" as a lone inventive genius. In the 1960s and 1970s, historians asserted that credit belonged to Edison's assistants, whose ideas he borrowed, perhaps stole. In *Thomas A. Edison and His Kinetographic Motion Pictures*, Charles Musser provides a balanced assessment. To be sure, Edison's experimenters were resourceful collaborators with valuable ideas of their own, but Edison coordinated their talents and made the enterprise work. As Musser explains, "It was Edison who gathered together and synthesized the key ideas that made possible the invention of motion pictures. He supplied the laboratory, the financing, the impetus, and the right personnel to help realize his vision." The three decades following Edison's bold announcement were years of inspiration and disappointment, public acclaim and cutthroat competition. And in 1918, only thirty years after his first experiments, Edison abandoned the motion picture business. What had happened? ◪ Charles Musser is uniquely qualified to tell this compelling story. This book draws on his three recent, critically acclaimed works, *The Emergence of Cinema: The American Screen to 1908* (Scribner's); *Before the Nickelodeon: Edwin S. Porter and the Edison Manufacturing Company* (University of California Press); and, with Carol Nelson, *High-Class Moving Pictures: Lyman H. Howe and the Forgotten Era of Traveling Exhibition, 1880-1920* (Princeton University Press). A filmmaker himself, Musser is Assistant Professor of Film Studies and American Studies at Yale University and has taught at Columbia University and New York University. ◪ Several others were instrumental in the publication of this book. Nancy Waters, Supervisory Museum Curator at Edison National Historic Site, served as project director, shepherding the book from manuscript to press; Edward Wirth, Assistant Archivist, and Douglas Tarr, Archives Technician at Edison, edited the text; and Nina Ovryn served as book designer. We thank them for their valuable contributions. Finally, we express our gratitude to the New Jersey Historical Commission for a generous grant that supported this project. ◪ The Friends of Edison National Historic Site are pleased to publish this important work which illuminates one of Thomas Edison's contributions to the making of popular culture.

THOMAS A. EDISON EXPERIMENTING WITH MICRO-PHOTOGRAPHY, A FIELD THAT COMPLEMENTED HIS WORK ON MOTION PICTURES. THIS PHOTOGRAPH WAS TAKEN BY W.K.L. DICKSON IN 1893.

Maryanne Gerbauckas
SUPERINTENDENT,
EDISON NATIONAL HISTORIC SITE

Wade Knowles
CHAIRMAN,
MOTION PICTURE
CENTENNIAL COMMITTEE,
FRIENDS OF EDISON NATIONAL
HISTORIC SITE, INC.

THOMAS A. EDISON
And His
KINETOGRAPHIC
MOTION
PICTURES

Introduction

The news was out. Front page headlines across the nation proclaimed: "Wizard Edison Weds Light to Sound," "The Kinetograph. Edison's Latest and Most Surprising Device." Thomas A. Edison had developed a way to show photographic images of people and things in motion. It was May 1891, and a new era of entertainment was about to begin.

Detail of film frames from Charles Batchelor's notebook, June 1891. The film subject, a man tipping his hat, appears to be identical to that shown to members of the Federation of Women's Clubs at the West Orange Laboratory on May 20, 1891.

The news broke in an unusual manner. Mina Edison, the inventor's wife, had been entertaining delegates to a convention of women's clubs at their home (Glenmont) in West Orange, New Jersey, on May 20th. Edison, just returning from a trip, led her guests down the hill to his laboratory and showed them his experimental motion picture device. A week later the women's group was replaced by a band of male reporters from the mass-circulation dailies. They came to see this latest invention to emerge from the inventor's bag of tricks. Though now in his mid-forties,

Edison "ran upstairs with the step of a boy" as the procession of journalists followed in his wake. In one of the experimental rooms on the second floor, he showed them a pine-box contraption attached to a phonograph. A reporter for the *New York Sun* peered into a small opening in the box and saw "a young fellow waving his hands and touching his hat. Sometimes he laughed or shook his head or twisted his body and wriggled around." The newsman was impressed: "Every motion was natural and perfect." The demonstration was, Edison assured his enraptured audience, only "the germ or base principle." It needed to be perfected, something he hoped to do in the following weeks.

Motion pictures were one of many new communication technologies to which Edison contributed his inventive talents. His earliest inventions improved the telegraph; the quadruplex, for example, permitted four messages to be sent over a single wire simultaneously. In the 1870s, he made important contributions to early telephone technology. Late in 1877, he invented the phonograph, which was marketed the following year as an entertainment novelty.

When Edison opened a new laboratory in West Orange, in late 1887, he was known as "the Wizard of Menlo Park"—Menlo Park, New Jersey, being the site of his former laboratory where the phonograph and electric light bulb had been invented. The nickname stuck, for people thought of Edison as a magician whose techno-

logical breakthroughs would transform their everyday lives. Of course, few Americans then enjoyed electric lighting, and the phonograph needed substantial improvement before it would achieve widespread use. But the promise was there; Edison was the symbol of an exciting new age.

Edison wanted his new laboratory to be a center for inventing. Here he and his fellow experimenters would improve existing products and create new ones. Factories would be built in the surrounding valley to manufacture these items for America and the world. To a large extent he succeeded. At his West Orange laboratory he revived the phonograph and turned it into a popular consumer product. He produced a successful nickel alkaline storage battery while losing large sums of money on iron ore milling. But the most successful product conceived and developed in his new "invention factory" was the motion picture.

DRAWING OF THE EDISON LABORATORY AND PHONOGRAPH WORKS IN WEST ORANGE, NEW JERSEY. THE BLACK MARIA IS AT THE UPPER CENTER OF THE PICTURE. PUBLISHED IN *EDISON PHONOGRAPH MONTHLY*, MAY 1903.

On Saturday, February 25, 1888, the well-known photographer Eadweard Muybridge gave an illustrated lecture at the Music Hall in nearby Orange, New Jersey. The high point of that evening's entertainment was the "zoopraxiscope." This strangely named device projected a sequence of still pictures onto a screen with such rapidity that they seemed to merge into a single moving image. Although based on a series of photographs taken by a group of cameras in rapid succession, the pictures had been hand-painted onto a circular plate of glass. They showed simple subjects such as a galloping horse and displayed a complete cycle of movement that could be repeated over and over again.

It is unknown whether Edison braved the bad weather to attend Muybridge's demonstration that night. However, two days later, the eccentrically mannered Muybridge visited Edison's laboratory to talk with America's most celebrated inventor. At this friendly meeting, Edison's motion picture invention may well have received its first spark. Muybridge suggested that they combine Edison's phonograph with his "zoopraxiscope." Together, they might be able to photograph and "phonograph" the famous Shakespearean actor Edwin Booth playing Hamlet. Edison approved of the idea but first turned to a more immediate task—the improvement of his phonograph.

EADWEARD MUYBRIDGE DEMONSTRATING HIS ZOOPRAXISCOPE GRACED THE COVER OF *THE ILLUSTRATED LONDON NEWS,* SATURDAY, MAY 25, 1889.

Edison and his colleagues with the "perfected" phonograph on which they had worked for three days with little rest. This photograph was taken by W.K.L. Dickson at 6:00 a.m. June 16, 1888. Surrounding Edison, who is seated at center, are (LEFT TO RIGHT) Fred Ott, Dickson, Charles Batchelor, A.T.E. Wangemann, John Ott, Charles Brown, and George Gouraud.

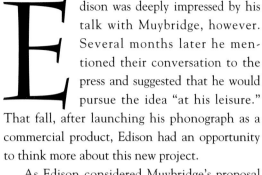

Edison was deeply impressed by his talk with Muybridge, however. Several months later he mentioned their conversation to the press and suggested that he would pursue the idea "at his leisure." That fall, after launching his phonograph as a commercial product, Edison had an opportunity to think more about this new project.

As Edison considered Muybridge's proposal more carefully, he saw its drawbacks. The photographer needed a different camera for each exposure. The painstaking transfer of each image to glass using nonphotographic processes was both expensive and time consuming. Edison's phonograph functioned much more cheaply and easily. The inventor thus concluded that he should develop his own, quite different, system for recording and "reproducing" visual reality.

On October 8, 1888, he wrote a "caveat" for the U.S. Patent Office. A "caveat" is a legal document in which the writer states that he is working on a particular invention in anticipation of filing a patent application. "I am experimenting upon an instrument which does for the Eye what the phonograph does for the Ear, which is the recording and reproduction of things in motion, and in such a form as to be both Cheap practical and convenient." The apparatus that captured these images would later be called "the kinetograph," the one that exhibited them would be "the kinetoscope."

Initially, Edison applied technological principles from his phonograph to his proposed motion picture invention. A series of minuscule photographs (1/32 of an inch wide), would spiral

A CYLINDER USED BY EDISON AND DICKSON IN THEIR EARLY EXPERIMENTS, CA. 1889; SHEETS OF PHOTOGRAPHIC FILM WOULD BE WRAPPED AROUND IT. THE CYLINDER FORM WAS A BASIC PART OF THE PHONOGRAPH, AND EDISON SIMPLY ADAPTED IT FOR MOTION PICTURES. THIS PARTICULAR ITEM, MOUNTED ON A BLOCK OF WOOD, SERVED AS EVIDENCE IN A LATER PATENT INFRINGEMENT CASE.

Monkeyshines, 1890.
THE FIRST MOTION PICTURE? AN
EDISON EMPLOYEE DRESSED IN
WHITE GESTURES BROADLY AGAINST
A BLACK BACKGROUND.

around a cylinder approximately three inches in diameter. These images would be taken by a single camera with a shutter opening and closing as the cylinder rotated past the lens. Once the photographic cylinder (containing 42,000 images) was developed and placed on the viewing device, the spectator could then look into a microscope and see a 28-minute movie while listening to the phonograph. If larger, transparent cylinders were used, Edison thought, the images might be projected onto a screen.

It all seemed possible—at least in theory. In practice there were problems. The images were too tiny and the curved surface rendered parts of the image out of focus. In February 1889, after further reflection and perhaps some initial experimentation, Edison wrote a second caveat which called for a cylinder with flattened surfaces. A third caveat, written early in the summer, suggested wrapping the cylinders with photographic film. The precise dates and sequence of experiments that led to Edison's invention of a modern motion picture system are shrouded in mystery. Existing records are fragmentary. One thing is evident: the inventor, hoping his patents would be upheld in the courts, subsequently claimed that certain events occurred earlier than they actually did.

William Kennedy Laurie Dickson, one of

CHARLES H. KAYSER, AN EDISON COLLEAGUE, WITH THE HORIZONTAL-FEED KINETOGRAPH, THE FIRST MOTION PICTURE CAMERA, CA. 1889-1890.

Edison's chief experimenters, was formally assigned to the project in June 1889. Although busy assisting Edison with other undertakings, Dickson was an accomplished photographer and the logical person to head the investigation. In many respects, the invention of Edison's motion picture system was a collaborative effort involving the different abilities of both Edison and Dickson. As we have already seen, Edison developed the initial idea and laid out basic principles that Dickson was assigned to implement. The sharing of ideas was crucial to the project's ultimate success.

As Dickson pursued the cylinder idea, he first used a photographic emulsion that adhered directly to the cylinder's surface. In following Edison's third caveat, he wrapped thin sheets of photographic film around the tube. Eventually Dickson adopted larger images—approximately 1/4 of an inch wide—but dispensed with the flattened surfaces called for in Edison's second caveat (these may have been intended only as a last-minute refinement once the basic principles were worked out). Surviving results from these cylinder experiments show an Edison employee dressed in white, placed against a black background and making an array of broad gestures or "monkeyshines."

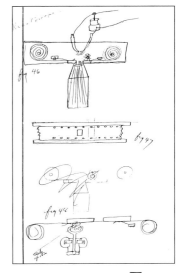

EDISON'S ILLUSTRATIONS FOR HIS FINAL MOTION PICTURE CAVEAT, WHICH HE PREPARED AFTER RETURNING FROM EUROPE WITH SOME NEW IDEAS, NOVEMBER 1889.

EXPERIMENTAL SUBJECT TAKEN BY W. K. L. DICKSON AND WILLIAM HEISE WITH THE 1891 HORIZONTAL-FEED CAMERA. THE SUBJECT IS JAMES DUNCAN, A DAY WORKER AT THE LABORATORY.

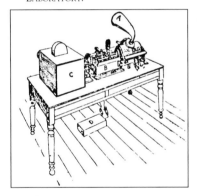

AN ILLUSTRATION OF EDISON'S EXPERIMENTAL KINETOSCOPE. *New York Sun*, MAY 1891.

Edison left for the Paris Exposition on August 3rd. In his absence Dickson pursued the cylinder experiments and constructed a small photographic building behind the main laboratory.

Meanwhile, Edison was fêted and introduced to Europe's leading citizens. One was Étienne-Jules Marey, who used photography to analyze the movement of birds and other animals. Working along more strictly scientific lines than Muybridge, Marey devised a single camera that made rapid, multiple exposures: paper film was advanced at regular intervals past the lens as a series of images was taken.

When Edison returned to the laboratory in October, Dickson had made only limited progress on his cylinder experiments. Within a month, Edison wrote a fourth and final motion picture caveat which proposed a totally different kind of kinetograph, one obviously influenced by Marey's work. A band of sensitive photographic film

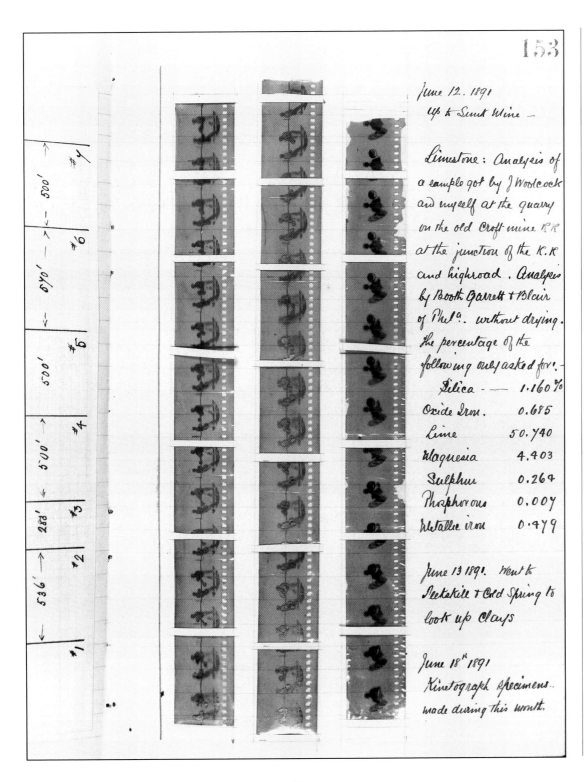

CHARLES BATCHELOR'S NOTEBOOK WITH SAMPLES OF NEGATIVES FROM EXPERIMENTAL MOTION PICTURE SUBJECTS, JUNE 1891. THE NOTES ON LIMESTONE PERTAIN TO EDISON'S ORE MILLING WORK; THE PAGE ILLUSTRATES EDISON'S SIMULTANEOUS INVOLVEMENT WITH SEVERAL RESEARCH PROJECTS.

would move behind the camera lens at the rate of 10 frames per second. In the same way, a developed film strip could be run through the apparatus and the images projected onto a screen. This caveat laid out the principles on which Edison's motion picture system would be based.

Edison, however, was always investigating several problems at any one time. Rather than pursue motion pictures, he turned his attention to another subject—improvements in iron ore milling—and took Dickson with him. It was not until October 1890 that Dickson returned to the motion picture problem. This time Edison teamed him with William Heise, who had experience making paper tape move through Edison's telegraph mechanisms. The sprightly Dickson and the heavy-set, slow-moving Heise must have made an odd couple. Together they worked on a kinetograph camera based on Edison's fourth caveat. The long film strips were 3/4 of an inch wide with images running along the film horizontally rather than vertically as they do today. A single row of small sprocket holes edged the top of the film strip.

By spring 1891, Edison's new approach had borne fruit; Dickson and Heise made short films of boxers and gymnasts and a close-up of a genial employee smoking a pipe. On May 20, 1891, Mina Edison and the participants at a Women's Clubs of America convention went to her husband's laboratory where they peered into a makeshift kinetoscope and enjoyed a brief glimpse of motion pictures. The device, Edison explained, had no value as a business machine but would amuse the public, allowing them to see *and* hear the famous Madame Adelina Patti sing "Home Sweet Home" for a nickel—while a ticket to her recitals cost five dollars.

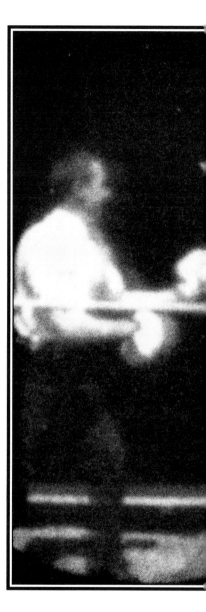

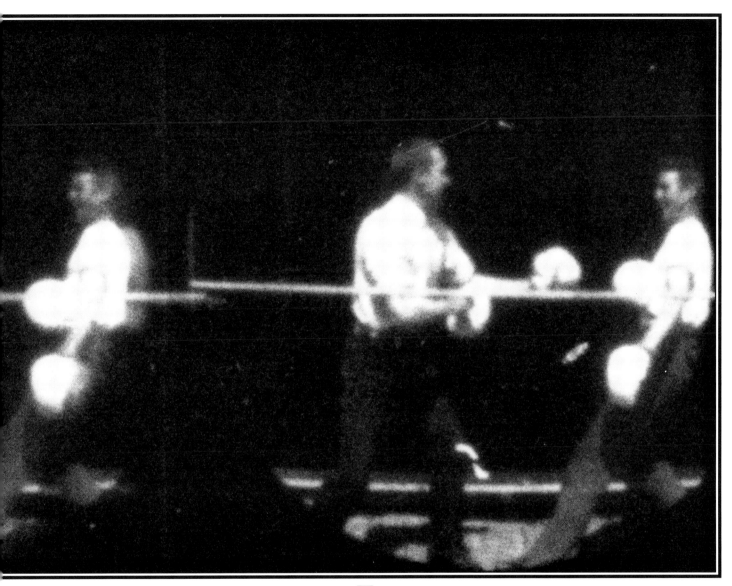

THIS SCENE OF MEN BOXING WAS SHOT BY
DICKSON AND HEISE, OPERATING WHAT WE
MIGHT CALL A MODERN MOTION PICTURE
CAMERA, IN LATE 1892.

B*LACKSMITH SCENE*
IS THE EARLIEST
KNOWN COMMERCIAL
MOTION PICTURE.
MADE IN THE
BLACK MARIA, THE
FILM WAS SHOWN AT
THE FIRST PUBLIC
EXHIBITION OF THE
KINETOSCOPE
ON MAY 9, 1893, AT
THE BROOKLYN
INSTITUTE OF ARTS
AND SCIENCES.

Although Edison's lawyers submitted patent applications based on the kinetograph's success, both Edison and Dickson recognized that the system needed refinement. A wider, tougher film and a vertical feed system were two of the improvements they worked out. This process took over a year and a half. By November of 1891, Dickson was placing orders for 1 1/2-inch wide film strips for this camera (essentially the format for today's 35mm motion picture film). However, it was not until late the following summer that Dickson and Heise were operating what we might call a modern motion picture camera. Images from the first frames of film were published that October; one set showed Dickson and Heise shaking hands, congratulating one another on their success. Two others were of men boxing and fencing against a black background. Even this camera needed further development; a kinetoscope that could exhibit approximately 50 feet of film had to be designed and built.

In December 1892, Edison began construction of a special motion picture studio designed by Dickson. This rectangular box-like structure,

about 48 feet long and 12 feet wide, was built by February 1893 but not completely outfitted until May. Covered in black tar paper, the building became known as the Black Maria, a slang expression for the police paddy wagons it was said to resemble. The roof could be opened and closed, and the entire structure turned on its axis. In this way, the stage area located at one end could receive the direct sunlight necessary for filming any time of the day. The Black Maria became the center of Edison's filmmaking activities for the next several years—perhaps between two and three hundred films were made within its walls before it became obsolete in 1900. The world's first specially built motion picture studio, it was torn down in 1903. At the suggestion of Edison's son Theodore, a full-scale working replica was built in 1954. This odd-looking building has been recently rehabilitated and is now used to demonstrate early filmmaking at Edison National Historic Site in West Orange, New Jersey

By April 1893 Dickson and Heise had filmed the first commercial motion picture subject in the Black Maria. *Blacksmith Scene,* which lasted

less than twenty seconds, showed three Edison employees hammering a piece of iron and then pausing to pass around a bottle of beer. The scene was a nostalgic look at work habits in an earlier America. This

film was shown at the first public exhibition of Edison's kineto- scope on May 9th, at a meeting of the Brooklyn Institute of Arts and Sciences. After hearing a brief illustrated lecture that described the invention, over 400 people lined up to take turns squinting into the peep-hole machine—a process that took several hours. As the demonstrator explained, projecting the image was not yet practical. Since the filmstrip in the kinetoscope was constantly moving, each frame was glimpsed for only the tiniest fraction of a sec-

ond. A projected image would have appeared hopelessly blurred, shaky, and faint.

The commercial exploitation of Edison's new motion picture system was delayed for another year. Plans to exhibit the kinetoscope that sum- mer at the Columbian Exposition in Chica- go fell through since the single proto- type shown in Brook- lyn could not be spared, and an initial order for twenty- five kinetoscopes was stalled. The Black Maria was used most- ly for experiments or publicity. *Edison Kinetoscopic Record of a Sneeze* was shot in early January 1894, to pro- vide illustrations for an article in *Harper's Weekly*. True filmmaking, though possible, was postponed.

WILLIAM HEISE AND W.K.L. DICKSON CONGRATULATING ONE ANOTHER ON THEIR WORK, 1892. SHOT WITH A MOTION PICTURE CAMERA THAT WOULD LOOK FAMILIAR TO US, AND USING 1 1/2" FILM THAT WAS SIMILAR TO TODAY'S 35MM FILM, THESE FRAMES ARE AMONG THE FIRST MODERN MOTION PICTURE FILMS.

Edison *Kinetoscopic Record of a Sneeze*, shot by Dickson in January 1894 and "starring" Fred Ott, one of Edison's colleagues, was made to provide illustrations for an article on motion pictures in *Harper's Weekly*.

CHAPTER 2
The Black Maria and Early Film Production
1894-1896

n April 1, 1894, Thomas Edison shifted the financial accounts for his motion picture activities from his laboratory to the Edison Manufacturing Company, a business enterprise which he completely owned. In many respects, this marked

the motion picture system's transformation from experiment to business enterprise. Through this date more than $24,000 had been spent on the development of motion pictures.* The system was now ready for commercial exploitation as an amusement novelty.

That same month Edison hired William Gilmore as general manager of the Edison Manufacturing Company. One of Gilmore's first acts was to deliver the first twenty-five kinetoscopes to a consortium of Edison's business associates and phonograph entrepreneurs (including the inven-

tor's personal secretary) for $250 each. Ten were installed at 1155 Broadway (near Herald Square), New York City, where Edison's motion picture novelty enjoyed an auspicious commercial debut on April 14th. Two more "kinetoscope parlors" were opened in Chicago and San Francisco during the following six weeks. People paid a nickel to see a short scene or, more typically, a quarter to see five.

Not only did each kinetoscope require a different subject, but return customers would demand new and different pictures. W.K.L. Dickson and William Heise, still responsible for Edison's motion

BUFFALO DANCE, 1894. NATIVE AMERICAN INDIANS FROM BUFFALO BILL'S WILD WEST SHOW BEFORE EDISON'S CAMERA IN SEPTEMBER.

---

* To translate such financial figures to 1990s prices, multiply dollar amounts by 12 to 15. Thus, in today's terms, this cost Edison over $300,000.

THE KINETOSCOPE PARLOR AT 1155 BROADWAY, NEW YORK CITY, OPENED APRIL 14, 1894. CUSTOMERS PAID A NICKEL TO SEE A SHORT SCENE, OR A QUARTER TO SEE FIVE. WITHIN SIX WEEKS, ADDITIONAL KINETOSCOPE PARLORS OPENED IN CHICAGO AND SAN FRANCISCO.

picture interests, had already begun serious film production. And filmmaking at the Black Maria often proved a diverting pastime, especially for Edison, who was disappointed by results of his iron ore milling efforts. On March 6th, Eugene Sandow, the world-famous strongman, came to the Edison laboratory. He stripped to a loincloth and then flexed his muscular torso for the camera. Edison, who had always enjoyed vaudeville and popular amusements of all kinds, appeared at the studio. While reporters looked on, the two famous personalities horsed around as Dickson took a few still photographs. The headline in one newspaper reported that the smartest man in the world had met the strongest.

In his public pronouncements, Edison had talked about filming the performances of famous opera singers or renowned actors. In practice, he and his male associates filmed typical examples of masculine amusements. *Cock Fight* showed two roosters engaged in a bloody battle. Spanish dancer Carmencita was the first of many women to pirouette for Edison's camera. Annabelle Whitford did Serpentine and Butterfly dances; she was so popular that she returned to the Black Maria many times between 1894 and 1897. In the late Victorian world, with its conservative mores, these early films captured activities largely forbidden to women and strongly opposed by church groups.

Edison's films often exposed middle-class women to this kind of entertainment for the first time.

Yet even in cosmopolitan Manhattan, there existed a need for film subjects that were less erotic and less violent. Films of two Scottish dancers doing a highland fling, an organ grinder, and trained bears were produced in time for the kinetoscope's New York debut. Dickson and Heise also took pictures of boxing cats and a wrestling dog from "Professor" Harry Welton's Cat Circus. Such films would also find favor in towns where the more risqué films were sure to be censored.

During the summer and fall of 1894, a stream of illustrious entertainers visited the Black Maria. Juan Caicedo, a headline attraction at Koster & Bial's Music Hall, walked a tightrope set up outside the Black Maria. The Glenroy brothers appeared in a burlesque boxing match. Buffalo Bill and a contingent of American Indians from his Wild West Show appeared before the camera in September. Annie Oakley also made a visit. As the theatrical season began, cast members performed highlights from successful Broadway plays and musicals. These were sold to kinetoscope owners for ten to fifteen dollars a film.

Edison initially sold kinetoscopes on a first-come, first-served basis; but this approach was disorganized and threatened to reduce profits. He therefore arranged with the men who had bought the first kinetoscopes to market the machines and films in the United States and Canada. This group formed the Kinetoscope Company, which was managed by Norman Raff and Frank Gammon. They purchased machines for $200 or $225 each and sold them for $350. A second group, headed by Franck (Franz) Z. Maguire and Joseph D. Baucus, formed the Continental Commerce

Eugene Sandow, the strongman, made his debut before the motion picture camera in March 1894. This souvenir card commemorates his appearance.

Annabelle Whitford performing A *Serpentine Dance*, 1894. She was one of Edison's most popular attractions.

Company and marketed the machine in Europe. By the fall of 1894 these companies were also responsible for helping Dickson secure appropriate subjects for filming.

The balance sheet for the Edison company's business year, which ended March 1, 1895, reveals the inventor's hefty profits from his moving picture novelty. Sale of kinetoscopes and films exceeded $180,000 with profits of roughly $89,000. Edison also paid generous royalties to Dickson and Heise for their key roles in the inventive process. During this period of economic recession, the visiting performers made the laboratory a happier place to work. They not only offered brief distractions but some lucky Edison employees received free passes to New York's leading shows. The excitement and energy continued into the new year.

But in early 1895, Edison's motion picture business began to sour as demand for kinetoscopes and films declined. New pictures lacked originality, and an attempt to revive interest with the Kinetophone, a combination kinetoscope and phonograph, proved a failure. Synchronization was imprecise and limited primarily to music accompanying dance numbers. Moreover, general manager William Gilmore had growing differences with W.K.L. Dickson, who resented what he saw as Gilmore's interference in the fledgling motion picture business. As Dickson grew unhappy, he shared technological secrets with ambitious competitors. In April 1895, he left the Edison laboratory and became one of the founders of the American Mutoscope Company, Edison's major competitor for the next fifteen years.

THE INTERIOR STAGE AREA OF THE BLACK MARIA WITH SEVERAL OF THE 'ACTORS' WHO APPEARED IN *BLACKSMITH SCENE*, CA. 1893.

THE "BLACK MARIA," THE WORLD'S FIRST STRUCTURE SPECIFICALLY DESIGNED AND BUILT AS A MOTION PICTURE STUDIO, AT THE WEST ORANGE LABORATORY, PHOTOGRAPHED BY W.K.L. DICKSON EARLY IN MARCH 1894. THE SLANTED ROOF OPENED TO ADMIT SUNLIGHT TO THE STAGE; THE ENTIRE STRUCTURE COULD BE TURNED ON ITS AXIS TO FOLLOW THE SUN THROUGHOUT THE DAY. THE CHICKEN COOP (*RIGHT, FOREGROUND*) HOUSES THE BIRDS THAT WILL STAR IN *COCK FIGHT*.

WILLIAM HEISE
FILMING IN THE BLACK
MARIA. THE PHONO-
GRAPH AT LEFT IS FOR
PUBLICITY AND EXPERI-
MENTAL PURPOSES ONLY.
THE ILLUSTRATION IS
FROM *CENTURY
MAGAZINE*, JUNE 1894.

*The Execution of Mary,
Queen of Scots,* 1895,
FEATURES ONE OF THE
FIRST SPECIAL EFFECTS IN
MOTION PICTURES.
HEISE AND ALFRED
CLARK, HIS NEW ASSOCI-
ATE, STOPPED THE CAM-
ERA AS THE SWORD
BEGAN TO FALL,
REPLACED "MARY"
(ACTUALLY PLAYED BY A
MAN) WITH A DUMMY,
AND RESUMED FILMING.
THE HEAD OF THE
DOOMED "QUEEN" FALLS
TO THE GROUND IN
WHAT APPEARS TO BE
ONE CONTINUOUS SHOT.

Although Heise shot a few new negatives, production virtually ceased after Dickson's departure. Then, in August, Raff and Gammon assigned one of their employees, Alfred Clark, to work with Heise and choose new subjects that would stimulate film sales. They produced several historical tableaux. In *The Execution of Mary, Queen of Scots,* Clark and Heise stopped the camera midway through the scene, substituted a dummy for the performer, and resumed filming as the sword descended and cut off the queen's head. This "stop-action" technique was used later in numerous trick films. Nonetheless, film sales continued to sag. Clark produced a few more dance pictures and then returned to the phonograph business. Raff and Gammon likewise were preparing to leave the motion picture business. Edison was in a quandary: despite efforts to provide added novelties, the kinetoscope's appeal had come to a quick and seemingly permanent end.

dison's motion picture business was revived by the introduction of projection. The idea of projecting motion pictures had occurred to thousands of people who peered into the kinetoscope; and a surprising number went on to pursue this goal. In retrospect, the

solution was obvious. A motion picture camera could have readily been converted into a projector, except that few people outside the Edison laboratory knew its inner workings. The peephole kinetoscope, as already pointed out, relied on a continuously moving band of film and a quickly rotating shutter. Projection could easily be achieved with the addition of an "intermittent," a mechanism that momentarily stopped each frame of film in front of the light source. This solution, however, eluded Charles Kayser, one of the Edison experimenters who had been assigned the problem.

The solution did not escape two aspiring inventors from Washington, D.C., Thomas Armat and C. Francis Jenkins, however.* They constructed a projector with an intermittent mechanism and called it the phantoscope. After giving several unsuccessful commercial exhibitions in October 1895, the young partners parted ways. Soon after, Armat demonstrated the projector to Raff and Gammon, who were extremely impressed. But the kinetoscope agents worried that Edison would see an outside alliance with

THE VITASCOPE ILLUSTRATED IN *SCIENTIFIC AMERICAN,* OCTOBER 31, 1896.

→+←

* During the course of 1895, machines for projecting motion pictures were independently developed in several industrial nations. Although Louis and Auguste Lumière's cinématographe, made in France, is best known, Max Skladanowsky built a projector in Germany and Robert Paul did so in England.

The May Irwin kiss, 1896. MAY IRWIN AND JOHN C. RICE TRAVELED TO THE BLACK MARIA IN WEST ORANGE TO RE-CREATE THIS MOMENT FROM The Widow Jones, A POPULAR MUSICAL COMEDY IN NEW YORK. THE BRIEF CLOSE-UP ENTER-TAINED MOVIE AUDIENCES FOR OVER A YEAR.

Armat as a betrayal. Perhaps only their desperate situation gave them courage to risk the inventor's displeasure. Even so, they waited more than a month, until January 15th, before meeting with Edison and Gilmore to raise the issue. In fact, Edison responded enthusiastically, eager to revive his failing enterprise. Raff and Gammon arranged for the Edison Manufacturing Company to build the projectors and supply the necessary films. Suddenly Edison was back in the motion picture business.

Having created the Edison-Armat alliance, Raff and Gammon headed the marketing effort that followed, moving quickly to outrun their competitors. From Edison they ordered eighty phantoscope projectors based on Armat's model. Only then did they discover that Armat had a rival co-inventor, C. Francis Jenkins, who was not a part of their agreements. To reduce their commercial vulnerability, Raff and Gammon renamed the projector, calling it the "vitascope." They also began to sell exclusive exhibition rights to entrepreneurs. Since Edison had previously promised his own projector, prospective investors were reluctant to invest in the vitascope. Raff and Gammon then proposed a promotional scheme that appeared to resolve this confusion. They asked permission from both Edison and Armat to advertise the projector as "Edison's Vitascope." In return, the Wizard would receive sums of money from the sale of exhibition rights. Since both wanted to see the vitascope succeed, they consented.

As Raff and Gammon's preparations for the vitascope moved forward, news of European showings of the Lumière cinématographe reached America. In Paris and London, audiences

THE VITASCOPE AT KOSTER & BIAL'S MUSIC HALL SHOWING ROBERT PAUL'S *ROUGH SEA AT DOVER*, APRIL-MAY 1896. WHILE THE FILM IS MERELY A SHOT OF WAVES CRASHING ON THE ENGLISH COAST, IT ASTONISHED EARLY MOVIEGOERS SIMPLY BY BRINGING NATURE INDOORS. THE INSET PICTURE SHOWS THE PROJECTION BOOTH.

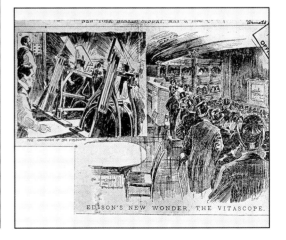

EDISON'S NEW WONDER, THE VITASCOPE.

THE NEWSPAPER CARTOONIST J. STUART BLACKTON MAKING A SKETCH OF EDISON IN THE FILM *INVENTOR EDISON SKETCHED BY WORLD ARTIST*, 1896. BLACKTON WOULD LATER BECOME A PARTNER IN THE AMERICAN VITAGRAPH COMPANY, ONE OF EDISON'S COMPETITORS. CAUGHT SELLING ILLEGAL COPIES OF EDISON FILMS, VITAGRAPH WOULD AGREE TO BECOME A LICENSEE FOR EDISON'S PATENTS.

❋❋

* The Music Hall was replaced by the Macy's department store early in this century.

cheered wildly as they saw outdoor scenes of a train pulling into a station and workers leaving a factory. Inevitably these foreign hits would soon reach the United States. Because it was crucial to sales that the American public see the vitascope as the origin of this newest motion picture fad, Raff and Gammon accelerated their plans to launch their projector. A private screening of the vitascope was held for Edison on March 27th, and he was extremely pleased with the results. The inventor happily played the familiar role of inventor-in-chief when the press attended a screening at his laboratory on April 3rd. Films of dancing girls were shown. A chortling journalist headlined his article: "Lifeless Skirt Dancers...Smirk and Pirouette at Wizard Edison's Command."

The vitascope premiered at Koster & Bial's Music Hall on Broadway and 34th Street, New York City, on April 23, 1896.* Six scenes were shown. Four films were holdovers from the kinetoscope era, including *Umbrella Dance*. A new subject, *The Monroe Doctrine*, dramatized a political cartoon which attacked British meddling in Venezuela. The hit of the evening, however, was not made at the laboratory. *Rough Sea at Dover*, which showed a wave coming toward the camera and crashing on the shore, had been produced by a British filmmaker, Robert W. Paul. Paul had shipped it to Edison with the hopes that they might come to some business arrangement. For several reasons, the film proved particularly effective. First, the vitascope showed 50-foot film loops over and over again at each screening. Thus the repetitive crashing of the waves on the shore mimicked the natural rhythm of the sea. Second, this large-scale image seemed to assault the spectator through its movement, emphasizing both cinema's life-like qualities and the ways it differed from reality (after all, motion picture waves never doused the spectators with water). Finally, the film brought inside something that could normally only be seen outside. In this it differed from scenes of dancing girls who could easily be seen right there on the stage.

The need for new, appealing subjects would be critical to the vitascope's success. May Irwin and John C. Rice went to the Black Maria in mid-April and performed their delicious kiss from *The Widow Jones*, a musical comedy then thrilling New York audiences. This close-up of a kiss remained a hit for the next year. Well before reports of the Lumières' cinématographe reached Edison's ears, his employees were working on a portable camera that would enable them to make motion pictures in distant locations. On May 11th, William Heise brought the camera to Herald Square and photographed the busy intersection from a second-story window. A week later it was shown in Koster & Bial's; people sitting inside the theater were delighted to see the bustling city outside.

James White, a former kinetoscope exhibitor, who joined Raff and Gammon in early April, started to work closely with Heise. The two filmed various city streets, Niagara Falls, and a planned head-on collision of two trains. Instead of bringing performers to the Black Maria, they now brought the camera to performers. The pair visited Coney Island where they filmed the famous Ferris Wheel, a horse race, and an Egyptian encampment. They also set up a makeshift studio on the rooftop of Raff and Gammon's New York City office building, sparing performers a commute to the West Orange studio. One particularly popular film showed newspaper cartoonist J. Stuart Blackton making a quick sketch of Edison.

During the summer of 1896, the Edison Manufacturing Company was the only film producer making a significant number of motion pictures in the United States. Nevertheless, the Vitascope Company encountered internal difficulties that limited its success. The demands of exhibitors for projectors and films far exceeded the supply. Furthermore, kinetoscope film, with a translucent base, was ill-suited for projection. When the Edison company ordered an appropriate clear-base film stock from its regular supplier (the Blair Camera Company), it met with disaster. After the film was developed, the emulsion quickly peeled off the celluloid base. Edison soon changed to film made by the Eastman Kodak Company, but exhibitors who had bought the bad prints were furious. Despite these difficulties, the Vitascope Company provided the first programs of projected motion pictures in numerous American cities, large and small. The vitascope, with its supply of Edison films, was enthusiastically hailed across the country.

"Edison's Vitascope" soon faced serious competition. The Lumière cinématographe had its New York (and United States) premiere in late June. By September more than a dozen cinématographes were playing in major cities. C.

Francis Jenkins, co-inventor of the phantoscope with Thomas Armat, was marketing his projector and duplicate copies of Edison films. Moreover, the American Mutoscope Company was showing W. K. L. Dickson's motion pictures in leading vaudeville theaters, while two other Edison employees had left and formed their own company (the International Film Company). They began by selling unauthorized copies of Edison productions but were soon filming their own pictures as well. European subjects, including those made by the Lumières, were being offered for sale. Foreign and domestic manufacturers also began to flood the market with projectors, many of them superior to the vitascope. Edison and Armat had yet to receive patents enabling them to challenge these rivals in the courts.

Forced to defend his place in the market, Edison restructured his business. The inventor severed his exclusive relationship with Raff and Gammon in late September and sold films to anyone who wanted them. The following month he hired away James White from Raff and Gammon. White became head of Edison's Kinetograph Department and enjoyed a salary of $100 a month plus a 5% commission on all film sales. Since White had worked closely with cameraman Heise in the previous months, their collaborative relationship continued much as before. To protect the resulting pictures from unauthorized duplication, Thomas Edison began to copyright the films in his own name.

The Edison company under White turned out a range of popular motion picture subjects. Many continued to show work-related activities: police drills in Central Park, employees leaving a Newark factory, and firemen racing to a fire. In December the company received a commission to take pictures that would promote the Lehigh

THE EDISON CAMERA CREW ON LOCATION PREPARING TO FILM A REMAKE OF *THE BLACK DIAMOND EXPRESS*, 1896, A FILM COMMISSIONED TO PROMOTE THE LEHIGH VALLEY RAILROAD. JAMES WHITE RESTS HIS ARM ON THE CAMERA; WILLIAM HEISE IS TO THE RIGHT. BELOW, A SCENE FROM THE COMPLETED FILM.

M*r. Edison at Work in His Chemical Laboratory, 1897.* STAGED IN THE BLACK MARIA, THIS FILM SHOWED THE INVENTOR ENGAGING IN SOME HUMOROUS SELF-PROMOTION.

Valley Railroad. Having a special train and several executives at his disposal, White shot *The Black Diamond Express* (showing this renowned express train racing toward, and past, the camera) and other scenes of the railroad, Niagara Falls, and Buffalo. One noteworthy subject, *Mr. Edison at Work in His Chemical Laboratory*, was shot in the Black Maria where a mock laboratory was constructed. The inventor flits from vial to vial concocting some potion that could well lead to another extraordinary breakthrough! Edison's sense of humorous self-promotion was never better demonstrated.

In the past Edison had made most of his motion picture profits from equipment (peep-hole kinetoscopes), not films. To maintain the profits

following the breakup with Raff and Gammon, Edison developed his own projector, soon known as the projectoscope or projecting kinetoscope. The first experimental model debuted in Harrisburg, Pennsylvania, on November 30, 1896, to great local acclaim. Other test models were gradually sold and that February the machine was placed on the commercial market for $100. Despite the new projector, films became Edison's principal source of profits, about $25,000 per year during 1896 and 1897. Although the prospects for Edison's motion picture business seemed bleak in late 1895, with the fading popularity of the peep-hole kinetoscope, filmmaking activities not only revived but expanded with the introduction of projection.

➤ CHAPTER 4 ➤
The Edison Company's Struggle to Survive
1897–1903

otion picture practices in the late 1890s were as different from today's methods as we can imagine. Today when we want to know who was responsible for a film, we usually ask who directed it. In the 1890s when people posed this question,

they were more likely to be asking about the exhibitor than the production company (the actual filmmaker was completely anonymous). How was this possible? The Edison Manufacturing Company and other production companies made short, one-shot films that usually lasted less than a minute (even the longest films ran under two minutes). Exhibitors selected and purchased these pictures, then organized them into programs. Some were miscellaneous collections of shots but others were built around a particular story or subject. Each exhibitor selected a differ-

ent group of films and sequenced them along somewhat different lines. Each showman wrote his own narration and delivered it each time these films were screened. Music and even sound effects were added to create a rich experience for the spectator. The exhibitor was often author, storyteller, and film editor combined. Today, looking at a few surviving films, we experience only the smallest taste of these popular shows.

The Edison company, in competition with other producers, provided raw material for the exhibitors' programs. In the summer

Wreck of the Battleship "Maine," 1898, BECAME AN IMMEDIATE HIT AND HELPED FUEL AMERICANS' WAR SENTIMENTS.

Burial of the "Maine" Victims, 1898. ALONG WITH Wreck of the Battleship "Maine," THIS PICTURE PROVED POPULAR WITH EXHIBITORS, WHO OFTEN EDITED SUCH FILMS INTO A NARRATIVE ACCOUNT OF THE SPANISH-AMERICAN WAR.

* Foreign patent offices would not have upheld Edison's claims since the key technological elements of his invention had been anticipated by others,

of 1897, James White and a newly hired cameraman, F. W. Blechynden, headed west on a filming expedition to California, Mexico, Japan, China, and Hawaii that lasted almost a year. Much of the filming was subsidized by railway and steamship companies eager to promote tourism. The more than 100 films taken during this trip were available for incorporation into evening-length travel programs.

The sinking of the Battleship *Maine* in Havana harbor on February 15, 1898, found James White in the middle of the Pacific Ocean heading toward China. As the incident moved the country toward war with Spain, the rival American Mutoscope Company sent two cameramen to Cuba where they filmed the wrecked *Maine* and other scenes that inflamed American patriotism when shown in vaudeville houses. Edison responded by making an exclusive arrangement with an independent cameraman, William Paley (no relation to the William Paley of CBS). The newspaper publisher William Randolph Hearst was already supplying Paley with transportation and a reporter, Karl Decker. Hearst, avid for war with Spain, recognized that motion pictures, in conjunction with his own newspapers' accounts of Spanish outrages, could incite Americans' jingoistic spirits. Paley filmed American warships off the Florida coast and entered Havana harbor where he finally succeeded in shooting *Wreck of the Battleship "Maine."* The pictures became immediate hits. When the war began, Paley returned to Florida and traveled with the troops to Cuba, filming *Roosevelt Rough Riders Embarking for Santiago,* and *Troops Making Military Road in Front of Santiago.* These and other subjects appeared on screens throughout the United States.

In addition to stepping up his efforts to provide more exotic and newsworthy films, Edison sought to improve his commercial position by enforcing the patents that he had finally been granted. By 1898 Edison, once the sole producer of motion pictures in the world, faced competition from domestic and European enterprises. He could do nothing about foreign rivals, since he had declined to file for motion picture patents abroad.* In the United States, however, he could use his mystique, his influence, and his lawyers' expertise to strengthen his commercial position. In August 1897, he received a camera patent on an application first submitted in August 1891. This allowed him to sue competitors for patent infringement. His legal offensive began in January 1898 and continued for several years. As a result, he was able to force a number of rival film companies out of business.

A handful of motion picture producers, however, challenged Edison's suits, including Sigmund Lubin in Philadelphia, William Selig in Chicago, and the American Mutoscope Company in New York City. Edison's principal court battle focused on the American Mutoscope Company, which had come to dominate the most lucrative parts of the motion picture business. Since it had developed a motion picture system somewhat different from Edison's and had been granted its own patents, an Edison victory in that battle would virtually assure his exclusive control of the motion picture business. This case, however, was not to be decided until the middle of 1901. Until then, the industry remained in considerable flux.

Rather than fight Edison in court, a few producers grudgingly agreed to recognize Edison's patents and become licensees. In the summer of 1898, the American Vitagraph Company—

owned by Albert E. Smith and J. Stuart Blackton (who had once sketched Edison's portrait for the inventor's camera)—was caught selling illegal copies of Edison films. The Vitagraph partners, who were also making their own pictures, agreed to become licensees and turn their negatives over to Edison for distribution. Many films produced by these licensees, particularly by Vitagraph and William Paley, were subsequently copyrighted in Edison's name before being offered for sale. The Edison company thus came to rely heavily on its affiliates for new subjects, particularly after William Heise left the motion picture business in the fall of 1898. In fact, James White was virtually the only Edison employee making films, despite his many other responsibilites as head of the Kinetograph Department.

During 1899 and 1900, James White produced a number of noteworthy Edison films. While most filmmakers were still making one-shot subjects, White experimented with multiple shots. For the *Shoot the Chutes* series he filmed the Coney Island amusement from three different camera positions. From a distant camera location, he photographed boats filled with thrill-seekers going down a ramp and into the water. He next placed the camera at the top of the ramp and finally in a boat traveling down the chute and into the pond. White's decision to combine these three different scenes into a single subject was suggested by the obvious interrelationship of the shots. Since single-shot films of this subject were common, White's multi-shot construction was something new.

Unlike Edison, most important film producers were also involved in exhibition. The Edison company's income was derived almost entirely from the sale of films and projectors. Edison's chief rival, renamed the American Mutoscope & Biograph Company, did not even sell films. Biograph made pictures for its own exhibition service, and this service was then made available to a vaudeville house or theater for a fixed weekly price. Producers of 35mm film like Vitagraph in New York and Lubin in Philadelphia operated exhibition services on a somewhat similar basis. Thus Blackton and Smith of Vitagraph only supplied Edison with negatives of their original comedies after these had played in the theaters using their service. Vitagraph made money by showing films, not by selling them.

Edison licensing methods often proved advantagous for all concerned. When a major news event occurred, like New York City's spectacular victory celebration for Admiral George Dewey in September 1899, James White coordinated cameramen from the various licensed companies so that all the most important locations were covered. Their negatives were then pooled and the films played New York vaudeville theaters serviced by Edison-licensed companies on the very day the pictures were shot. Afterwards, Edison reaped profits by selling copies to unaffiliated exhibitors.

Licensing arrangements eventually benefited the licensees more than Edison himself. When the inventor sought to extract a more satisfactory royalty from their exhibition incomes, the licensees resisted. Early in 1900, after Vitagraph threatened to sue Edison for breach of contract, the inventor revoked the company's license. The resulting legal wrangle reflected poorly on all parties, although Vitagraph was relicensed in the fall of 1900.

From early 1898 through early 1901, the Edison company struggled to find its way. Motion picture profits from film and projectors

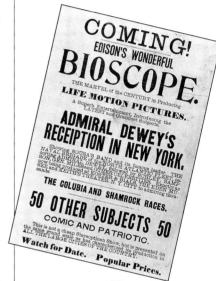

BROADSIDE FOR A TRAVELING MOTION PICTURE EXHIBITOR SHOWING FILMS OF "ADMIRAL DEWEY'S RECEPTION (SIC) IN NEW YORK." THESE SCENES WERE SHOT ON SEPTEMBER 30, 1899, DURING THE DEWEY HOMECOMING PARADE FOLLOWING THE SPANISH-AMERICAN WAR.

fluctuated between $22,000 and $28,000, the amount generally falling as the century ended. Edison again found his motion picture business in a precarious position. In mid-1900 he arranged to sell his film patents and business to Biograph, but the financing unexpectedly fell through. Biograph tried to extend the deadline, but Edison refused and instead renewed his commitment to motion pictures.

Edison had to change in order to remain competitive; his motion picture equipment needed upgrading; the Black Maria was too far from the necessary talent and supplies (backdrops, costumes, props, etc.) for filmmaking. In November, James White and William Gilmore hired Edwin S. Porter, an experienced exhibitor and equipment builder, for fifteen dollars per week. They also rented offices at 41 East 21st Street, New York City, and built a glass-enclosed studio on the roof. This studio could be used year-round and was superior to any then available in the United States. Pictures would be made in New York, but the printing and other laboratory work would be done at Edison's facilities in West Orange.

The Twenty-first Street studio was completed in January and ready for business by February 1901. To run its new studio, the Edison company assigned the role of motion picture photographer to Edwin Porter and hired George S. Fleming, an actor and scenic designer, to direct. Working together these two turned out a variety of comedies, some of them adaptations of newspaper cartoons. Other pictures reenacted distant news stories. When a news event such as President McKinley's second inaugural occurred, White and Porter traveled to Washington, D.C., and filmed it.

Edison's fortunes reached a high point on July 15, 1901, when the U.S. Circuit Court declared that Biograph was infringing the inventor's patents. Biograph appealed, and the company was allowed to continue only limited operations under court supervision. Rival Sigmund Lubin's cameraman, Jacob (James) B. Smith, joined the Edison staff; aware of the information Smith could share with Edison and fearing more litigation, Lubin fled the country. Edison business executives, feeling more secure about their own filmmaking abilities, had already withdrawn Vitagraph's license for a second time. The Vitagraph partners could no longer make films, only show them. Only William Selig, a Chicago producer, escaped legal restraint, but his future was linked to the fate of Biograph's appeal. Edison's triumph had closed down or curtailed much of the American film industry. With competition reduced, his business prospered, though the industry as a whole suffered.

Given its new position, the Edison Manufacturing Company avoided unnecessary investment and reduced the number of pictures made in its studio. James White and his crew concentrated much of their energy on filming at the Pan-American Exposition in Buffalo. In early September, they returned to document President McKinley's visit to the exposition. There they filmed him giving his last speech. The next day the cameramen were standing outside the Temple of Music when McKinley was assassinated inside. They went on to film the President's elaborate funeral in Buffalo, Washington, and Canton, Ohio.

Porter and Fleming then made a four-shot dramatization of the assassin's death, *The Execution of Czolgosz*. The film was notable for combining multiple interior and exterior shots to depict a single locale. The first two scenes

The Execution of Czolgosz, 1901, RE-CREATED THE EXECUTION OF PRESIDENT MCKINLEY'S ASSASSIN. THE FILM OPENED WITH EXTERIOR SHOTS OF AUBURN STATE PRISON, THUS CREATING THE ILLUSION THAT THE DRAMATIZED EXECUTION WAS ACTUALLY TAKING PLACE WITHIN THE PRISON.

showed the actual exteriors of Auburn State Prison where Czolgosz was executed. The next two, made back in the studio, showed the prison interior as (1) Czolgosz was taken from his cell and (2) led into the execution chamber and electrocuted. Although editorial control was gradually shifting from exhibitor to producer, in this case showmen were given the choice of buying the film without the opening panoramic views of the prison.

The films related to the Pan-American Exposition and the McKinley assassination

enjoyed tremendous sales over the next several months. Despite the boon, Edison's Kinetograph Department invested little in further film production. Then in March 1902, the Court of Appeals reversed the lower court's ruling against Biograph. Edison's patents were declared invalid; their claims were too broad. Edison had to apply for a patent reissue. In the meantime, Lubin, Vitagraph, and others were free to resume their activities. All court cases against them would have to be started from scratch.

To meet the renewed competition, Edison's

EDWIN S. PORTER'S *JACK AND THE BEANSTALK*, 1902. JACK SELLS THE COW FOR A HATFUL OF BEANS. INFLUENCED BY THE WORK OF THE FRENCH FILMMAKER GEORGES MÉLIÈS, THIS TEN-SCENE VERSION OF THE FAIRY TALE IS SMOOTHLY DEVELOPED AND EASILY UNDERSTOOD, NOTABLE ADVANCES OVER EARLIER FILMS

PORTER'S *How They Do Things on the Bowery,* 1902, TELLS THE FAMILIAR STORY OF THE COUNTRY BUMPKIN IN THE WICKED CITY. THE BARTENDER EJECTS THE FARMER FROM THE SALOON. IN THE NEXT SHOT, THE SAME ACTION REPEATED AS THE POLICE STAND OUTSIDE AND OBSERVE THE FARMER'S LANDING ON THE STREET. SHOWING ONE ACTION FROM TWO POINTS OF VIEW WAS AN INNOVATION AT THE TIME.

Kinetograph Department undertook more ambitious productions. The Frenchman Georges Méliès, in particular, had demonstrated the popularity of story films. Now Porter and Fleming explored this route with four pictures made during the rest of the year. *Appointment by Telephone* was a three-shot, risqué comedy with a simple beginning, middle, and end. It was followed by the ten-shot, 12-minute *Jack and the Beanstalk,* a fairytale film in the Méliès tradition. Both films presented smoothly developed, easily understood stories—notable advances over anything previously made in the United States.

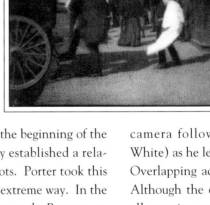

Porter, who was increasingly in charge of the Edison studio, was impressed by the storytelling technique of another Méliès film, *A Trip to the Moon,* based on a Jules Verne story. A rocket full of scientists lands on the moon at the end of one shot and then lands again at the beginning of the next. This repetition clearly established a relationship between the two shots. Porter took this idea and applied it in a more extreme way. In the comedy *How They Do Things on the Bowery,* an unsuspecting farmer comes to the city and is tricked by a wily prostitute. In a saloon, she gives him a Mickey Finn, steals his valuables, and leaves. The bartender, finding his customer unable to pay, kicks him and his suitcase out the door. The third shot shows the saloon exterior where the police arrive and wait until the farmer and his suitcase are tossed onto the street. The last two scenes show the same time span twice—first from one vantage point and then from the other. Today a filmmaker would cut back and forth between these two locations as the action developed, but in 1902 this use of repetition not only seemed logical but a bold innovation.

Porter's method of storytelling was more successfully realized in *Life of an American Fireman,* made between November 1902 and January 1903. This story, of a fireman who rescues a woman and a child from a burning building, embodied key representational techniques that characterized cinema for the next five years. The final rescue is shown twice, first from the inside of the burning house and then from the outside. The panning camera follows a fireman (played by James White) as he leaps off the fire engine as it arrives. Overlapping actions occur at almost every edit. Although the exhibitor had not yet surrendered all creative responsibility, Porter had asserted control over the editing and demonstrated that such control permitted even greater artistic expression. He thus established himself as America's preeminent filmmaker—and Edison as the preeminent American producer—of the new century.

American filmmaking proceeded fitfully during the first years of the twentieth century. Because Sigmund Lubin had been selling duplicates of Edison films after reopening for business, the inventor sued the Philadelphia producer for copyright

infringement. No sooner had *Life of an American Fireman* been completed than the courts declared Edison's method of film copyright invalid. (The judge wanted each frame of film submitted separately, a hopelessly time consuming and expensive task!) Without legal protection for his investment, Edison halted serious film production for five months and dismissed the stage director George Fleming. Meanwhile, the energetic James White was replaced by William H. Markgraf, William Gilmore's brother-in-law. Porter did not resume filmmaking until that sum-

mer, after a higher court reversed the earlier decision and upheld Edison's procedure for copyrighting films.

The Edison company continued to produce a wide variety of subjects: news films, travel subjects, comedies, novelties, and story films. Some offered notable innovations. *Uncle Tom's Cabin* (July 1903) was the longest film yet made by the company. To produce this 20-minute version of the famed theatrical melodrama, Edwin Porter hired a traveling troupe that regularly performed the play and used their sets and staging. *The Gay*

THE COVER OF EDISON FILM CATALOG FOR *Uncle Tom's Cabin*. WHEN THIS WAS RELEASED IN JULY 1903, IT WAS THE LONGEST FILM YET MADE BY THE COMPANY.

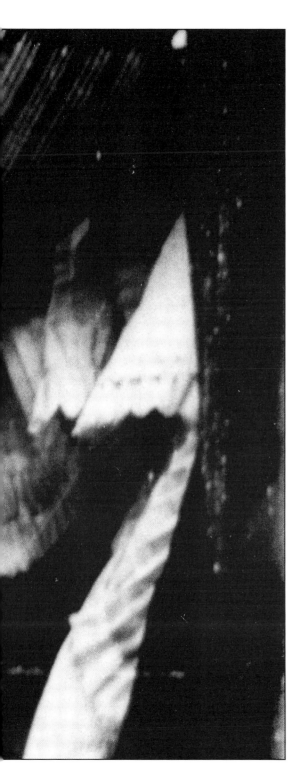

Shoe Clerk was only a single brief scene, but it includes an innovative close-up. Like many gag films from this period, this one played with both sexual desire and punishment for violating social codes. The shoe clerk flirts with the female customer and ultimately gets bashed by her elderly chaperone.

The Edison Manufacturing Company continued its extensive output into the fall when Porter began work on *The Great Train Robbery* (November 1903), the first blockbuster in motion picture history. It was directly inspired by several violent crime films coming out of England—pictures like A *Daring Daylight Burglary* and *Desperate Poaching Affray*. The Edison film depicted a carefully planned train hold-up, the bandits' getaway, a posse hunt, and the final shoot-out in which the bad guys are killed. Despite the western locale, the picture's exteriors were all shot in New Jersey. The train passengers held up by the bandits were Edison employees; the wooded scenes were shot at South Mountain Reservation near the laboratory, and the train scenes on the Lackawanna Railroad. G. M. Anderson, who subsequently became the world-famous cowboy star "Bronco Billy," played several small roles in the film (he is the passenger shot in the back trying to escape) and assisted Porter with the direction. The picture was immediately booked in all the leading vaudeville theaters in New York and soon appeared throughout the

THE GAY SHOE CLERK, 1903, ANOTHER INNOVATIVE FILM, CUTS FROM THE FULL (OR ESTABLISHING) SHOT TO A CLOSE-UP (*left*) OF THE CLERK

FITTING THE WOMAN'S SHOE AND BACK TO THE FULL SHOT— UNUSUAL AT A TIME WHEN MOST FILMS WERE COMPOSED ENTIRELY OF FULL SHOTS.

The cover of Edison film catalog No. 201, featuring *The Great Train Robbery*, 1903, the first blockbuster motion picture. The film was featured by traveling showmen for several years and was often the first attraction in the new nickelodeons. It remains to this day the most well-known Edison film.

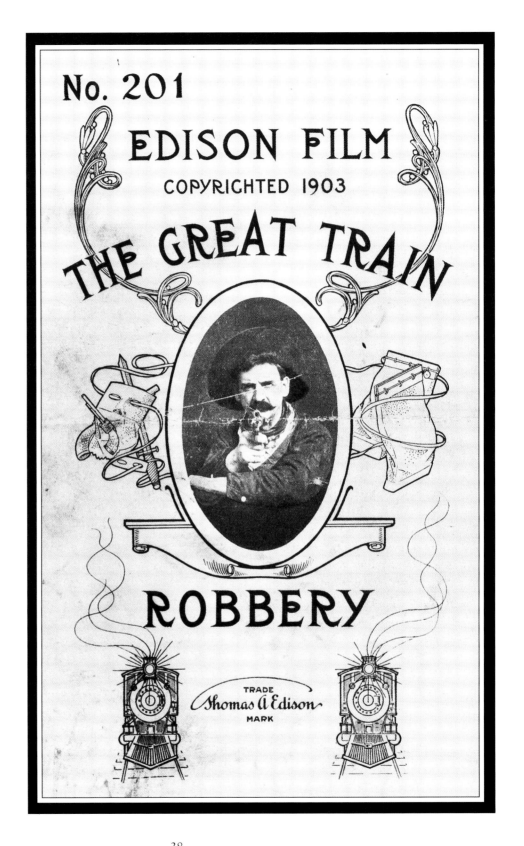

country. It remained the most popular motion picture for several years and was often the first picture to be shown in the small "nickelodeon" theaters that began to pop up across the country in 1905-06.

Although *The Great Train Robbery* offered an obvious recipe for success and Edwin Porter was rewarded with a raise (to $35 a week!), the Edison company did not immediately make another film of this type. Edison executives insisted on producing a wide range of subjects and often encouraged Porter to remake the hit pictures of the company's American competitors. In addition, Edison and other American film companies purchased uncopyrighted films abroad, shipped them to the United States, made cheap duplicates, and sold these to the domestic market. But this profitable and legal (if somewhat unethical) business became increasingly impractical as two prominent European producers, Georges Méliès and Pathé Frères, opened New York offices and took steps to end the "pirating."

Thomas Edison's precise involvement in business decisions of this period is not known. Certainly, all important decisions had his approval and many of these may have been initiated by him or made jointly with William Gilmore. Alex T. Moore, who took over as head of the Kinetograph Department in 1904, was also involved in the process.

As the year 1904 neared its end, the Edison Manufacturing Company introduced two significant developments. First, story films became the dominant product. Although acted films had generally sold better than "actualities" (nonfiction films, often of everyday activities or news events), they were also much more expensive to make. Edison had felt reluctant to make the necessary large-scale investment until 1904, when the much higher financial return clearly justified the switch. Second, Porter was given greater latitude to make original subjects rather than imitate other producers' successes. Both moves displayed Edison's confidence in the growing profitability of moving pictures. The hiring of Wallace McCutcheon in May 1905 was further evidence of this faith. Edison executives snatched McCutcheon from the Biograph company, where he had been its chief motion picture producer. The move was undoubtedly designed to injure a rival. But Porter had always preferred to work closely with a collaborator (such as Fleming), and McCutcheon's presence inaugurated a somewhat similar co-director relationship.

Even before McCutcheon arrived, Porter initiated a series of fresh, compelling story films. Several explored important social problems and sympathized with the Progressive movement's demand for social, economic, and political reforms. In *The Kleptomaniac* (February 1905),

The Great Train Robbery, THE SHOOTOUT IN THE STATIONMASTER'S OFFICE.

The *Kleptomaniac*, 1905. MRS. BANKER GOES ON A SHOPLIFTING SPREE IN MACY'S; THE DESPERATE MOTHER SPONTANEOUSLY STEALS BREAD FOR HER CHILDREN. IN THE COURTROOM, JUSTICE FAVORS THE RICH. THE EDISON COMPANY FOUND THAT FILMS DEALING WITH SOCIAL ISSUES WERE LESS POPULAR THAN MELODRAMAS.

Mrs. Banker steals expensive baubles from Macy's while a desperately poor mother with two young children and no husband steals a basket of food left unattended on the street. Both are arrested; however, Mrs. Banker is ultimately freed since her "kleptomania" is a psychological problem while the poor woman is sent to jail. In fact, the film would seem to suggest that Mrs. Banker's stealing is not unlike the activities of her husband. (Bankers were frequently attacked by Progressives for their role in financing gigantic corporations.) *The Ex-Convict* (December 1904) treats sympathetically a man struggling to make a living.

Other films, such as *The Train Wreckers* (1905), create a simple opposition between good guys and bad guys in which criminals seek to destroy society. Some pictures resort to racial and ethnic stereotypes typical of the period. In *Stolen by Gypsies* (1905), the gypsies kidnap a child apparently because this is what gypsies do.

Sales figures indicate that simple melodramas, comedies, and trick pictures did better in the marketplace than social issue dramas. *The Train Wreckers* sold 157 copies in 1905-06 while *The Kleptomaniac* sold only 28. Soon Porter and McCutcheon avoided the more controversial and less profitable subjects; comedies predominated, buttressed by a few melodramas. *The Terrible Kids* (1906) was part of the immensely popular "bad boy" genre. It showed two boys and their faithful dog annoying the adult world with a series of pranks. In *Life of a Cowboy*, the picture that Porter always maintained was "the first western," a cowboy saves a young woman from a band of outcasts and then settles down to adult responsibilities. Both sold well over 100 copies each. *Dream of a Rarebit Fiend* (1906), a comedy using a variety of camera tricks, sold an astounding 192 copies in the year it was released.* With the proliferation of nickelodeon theaters in 1906, Edison film sales on a per film basis roughly doubled from the previous year.

The Edison company, after surviving several years of despair and disruptions, saw profits from films move steadily upward from almost $25,000 in 1903-04 to just under $100,000 in 1906-07.** Profits from sales of projectors multiplied almost six-fold to $87,000, reflecting the boom in motion pictures. Yet success created its own kind of problems. The Twenty-first Street facility was cramped and not amenable to expansion. On June 20, 1905, the Edison company bought a plot of land in the Bronx to build a new studio. It had offices, dressing rooms, substantial storage space, a large glass-enclosed area for filming, and facilities for developing the negative film. Work was scheduled to begin at Christmas time and end the following spring; however, delays postponed completion until July 1907.

Preparations for a move to the new studio coincided with a personnel change. Wallace McCutcheon left Edison in May 1907 and was replaced by J. Searle Dawley, a stage manager and writer for the Brooklyn-based Spooner Repertory Company. He became Porter's contact with the theatrical world, collaborating on scripts and working with the actors. Porter was the senior filmmaker of the pair, and little changed from earlier pictures in terms of subject matter, storytelling methods, or production organization.

In some respects, the studio provided Porter with new freedom. As early as *A Race for Millions* (August-September 1907), he constructed an elaborate Wild West town inside the studio—complete with gun duel and a car driven onto the set. Nevertheless, the intense demands for new

A NEW STUDIO IN THE BRONX REPLACED CRAMPED QUARTERS ON 21ST STREET IN 1907. THE NEW FACILITY HAD AMPLE ROOM FOR OFFICES, STORAGE, DRESSING ROOMS, FILM DEVELOPING LABS, AND A LARGE GLASS-ENCLOSED SPACE FOR FILMMAKING.

* Even today only 200 film prints would be made for a picture given a broad, nationwide release.
** Each business year ran from March 1 to the end of the following February.

A *Race for Millions*, 1907, FEATURED AN ENTIRE WESTERN TOWN BUILT INSIDE EDISON'S BRONX STUDIO.

product created commercial pressures that made it more and more difficult for Porter to work as he wished. The rate of production increased steadily from two pictures per month in August to four per month by March 1908, when the studio was finally in full working order. By that time, the Edison Manufacturing Company was releasing a new film each week. This meant that film production was driven by deadlines. In the past, Porter had often worked on a picture until he felt it was properly finished. That luxury ceased when he had to meet a predetermined release schedule.

While Edison filmmaking had become more elaborate, few of its essentials had changed since *Life of an American Fireman* made five years earlier. The family-centered drama *Rescued from an Eagle's Nest* (January 1908) displayed the same cinematic techniques as the earlier film, techniques applauded in 1903, but simply old-fashioned by 1908. Yet *Rescued from an Eagle's Nest* was notable for its male lead, D. W. Griffith, who was then an occasional actor for both the Edison and Biograph companies. Within six months, Griffith would become a director at Biograph and quickly develop a set of modern storytelling conventions.

✦ CHAPTER 6 ✦
Edison's Search for Commercial Stability
1908-1912

E ven with his new studio in operation, Edison faced severe competition from Pathé Frères in France and Vitagraph in the United States. Both boasted substantially larger outputs and their storytelling methods were noticeably more advanced. Several other producers

had equalled Edison's output—including Sigmund Lubin, William Selig, and Biograph. Even more seriously, new companies were beginning to spring up in the United States—notably the Kalem Company, based in New York, and the Essanay Film Manufacturing Company of Chicago. Each was started by two or three men who combined experience in distribution and production. Almost as troubling for Edison's future, foreign motion picture producers from half a dozen countries were flooding the American market with their films. In fact, the American screen was dominated by European pictures.

Edison's main hope for regaining a prominent commercial position was to sue rivals for patent infringement. After the higher court had invalidated Edison's original motion picture patents, new ones had been issued in 1902 and again in 1904. Between 1902 and 1905, Edison again sued virtually all American motion picture producers for patent infringement. In March 1907, Edison and his reissued patents finally won a partial victory in the Court of Appeals. Although the defendant, Biograph, had a distinctive system that did not infringe the inventor's patents, the court declared, other cameras did. Edison promptly reactivated a longstanding suit against Selig in the Chicago courts and won another victory in October 1907.

The time for rival film companies to negotiate with Edison had arrived. The outcome of futher legal fighting might be uncertain, but a sharp, if brief, depression and the threat of increased competition made all established producers ready to cooperate. In private meetings, Edison's lawyers and executives soon asserted their authority. They insisted that production companies would have to be licensed and pay a half-penny royalty on each foot of motion picture film that they sold. In return, Edison would license only seven producers: all others would presumably be forced out of business either legally or commercially. Pathé, Méliès, Selig, Lubin, Vitagraph, Kalem, and Essanay signed up but Biograph refused. It created a rival and much smaller organization relying heavily on the product of excluded foreign producers.

The Association of Edison Licensees began official operations on March 1, 1908, and spent the next several months warring with Biograph in every way legally imaginable. The two organizations sued each other and those film exchanges and theaters serviced by the rival. They cut prices. They maligned each other in the press. Yet the smaller Biograph company survived and even showed signs of prospering as D. W. Griffith began to direct its films. Biograph further strengthened its position by allying itself with Thomas Armat, who controlled significant projection patents. Pressure existed on all sides for a settlement. Biograph wanted equal recogni-

tion and a share of the royalties.

In June, Thomas Edison replaced William Gilmore; Frank Dyer, who had headed his legal staff for many years, became vice-president of the Edison Manufacturing Company while Charles H. Wilson was appointed general manager. Dyer now took charge of the negotiations. After many difficulties, agreement was finally reached among Edison, Biograph, and the licensed producers who had to approve any changes to the existing agreement.

On December 18, 1908, Edison and Biograph formed the Motion Picture Patents Company which assumed ownership of all Edison, Biograph, Armat, and Vitagraph patents. The Patents Company then licensed all former Edison licensees plus Edison and Biograph. In addition, George Kleine was licensed to import two reels of film per week, one made by Gaumont in France, the other by Urban-Eclipse (an English-led undertaking). Both European producers controlled significant patents and it was imperative that they not be excluded from what became known as "the Trust." Film exchanges were also licensed, but the terms put the producers firmly in control. Likewise, the Trust made an arrangement with the Eastman Kodak Company: it would buy all its film from Eastman if Eastman would not sell to those outside the Trust. Eastman collected royalties on film purchases, which were then handed over to the Patents Company for division among its members. Furthermore, each theater was now required to pay a two-dollar royalty on the projection patents if it wanted to show licensed films. This combination of interlocking agreements was expected to vanquish all opposition and produce a large income independent of actual filmmaking.

While highly successful for a time, the Motion Picture Patents Company did not fully

FILMING A COUNTRY GIRL'S SEMINARY LIFE AND EXPERIENCES INSIDE EDISON'S NEW STUDIO IN MARCH 1908.

EXECUTIVES OF THE COMPANIES LICENSED BY THE MOTION PICTURE PATENTS COMPANY GATHER AT THE EDISON LABORATORY ON DECEMBER 18, 1908. FIRST ROW (L. TO R.): FRANK L. DYER, SIGMUND LUBIN, WILLIAM T. ROCK, THOMAS A. EDISON, J. STUART BLACKTON, JEREMIAH J. KENNEDY, GEORGE KLEINE, AND GEORGE K. SPOOR. SECOND ROW: FRANK J. MARION, SAMUEL LONG, WILLIAM N. SELIG, ALBERT E. SMITH, JACQUES A. BERST, HARRY N. MARVIN, THOMAS ARMAT (?), AND GEORGE SCULL (?).

succeed. Many owners of film exchanges, including Carl Laemmle (future president of Universal), were displeased with their reduced role. They left the Trust and began producing films on their own. Nevertheless, the Motion Picture Patents Company and its licensed producers initially controlled from 75% to 90% of the American market. Edison was guaranteed substantial royalties and his motion picture company had a golden opportunity to reap huge profits. Profits from projector sales almost tripled to more than $220,000 for the 1907-08 business year. Although film profits changed little for the same period, they doubled to $230,000 in 1908-09, reflecting an increased level of production at the new studio. Nonetheless, other companies quickly expanded production, and their output was often more popular than Edison films. Edison pic-

tures retained only 8% of the market in June 1908. To further increase its output, the Kinetograph Department formed a second production unit. It was headed by J. Searle Dawley and Fred S. Armitage, an experienced cameraman who had worked extensively for Biograph. Edwin Porter both ran the studio and directed films for the first unit. To accommodate this expansion (and to anticipate future growth), the Bronx studio was enlarged. By September, Edison was releasing two reels (2,000 feet) of film each week—an increase of more than 400% in a single year.

Although Edison pictures from this period do not survive, reviews and a few film fragments indicate that the company was failing to keep up with its competitors. The pressure to increase output may have weakened the quality of the films, but, more importantly, little changed in Porter's repertoire of cinematic techniques. In contrast, the more advanced companies were revising their storytelling methods. The films were more comprehensible and the performances more restrained and "true to life." The public's expectations were thus changing, to Edison's disadvantage. In a typical review, one Edison film was called "a confused, unintelligible series of scenes." Since the inventor held weekly film screenings in his laboratory library, he and his management team were well aware of the problems.

The Edison Manufacturing Company was trying desperately to improve its pictures by the end of 1908. Dyer and Wilson were actively searching for skilled directors from France. Finally they restricted Porter's responsibilities to that of studio head and hired H. C. Matthews as director. Henry Cronjager, Porter's assistant, was elevated to cameraman. But the key to better films was not found (if anything, reviews suggest that they got worse). The failing was not simply one of storytelling technique. It was also one of organizing production. Dyer and Wilson restructured the production units, giving the director principal responsibility. If one person were clearly in charge of a picture, then it would be clear whom to reward and whom to blame. But the plan met with resistance and destroyed the collaborative relationship that had existed between director and cameraman.

Porter was unhappy with Edison's new organization of production and proved uncooperative. By the end of February, Edison and his executives had had enough. Alex T. Moore was fired and Porter was removed from any position of significant responsibility. Horace G. Plimpton, who lacked any background in motion pictures, was brought in as studio chief, replacing Porter. Although Edison filmmaking was at a low point, production expanded; a third unit was added in March and a fourth that June.

The rapid increase in film production necessitated other important changes. Dawley gradually developed a core group of reliable actors. They appeared regularly in Edison productions—at least when their film work did not conflict with appearances on the stage. All received five dollars a day, regardless of the roles they played. Justus D. Barnes, who had played the bandit chief in *The Great Train Robbery*, was hired in August 1908 to work for the Kinetograph Company on a full-time basis. Augustus Balfour and Francis Sullivan followed later in the year. As Laura Sawyer and others were hired full-time in the spring of 1909, a stock company of actors took shape. For a time, the certainty of regular work reduced salaries—usually fifteen dollars per week instead of five dollars a day. But by the second half of 1909, the more prominent players were receiving thirty dollars or thirty-five dollars a week. Competition from theater—and perhaps other film companies—pushed salaries upward. Cameramen received slightly less, while directors averaged about forty dollars per week. Plimpton was at the top, making one-hundred dollars per week.

As the movies became an increasingly prominent part of American life, Thomas Edison had to pay greater heed to society's evolving attitudes toward this new form of entertainment. After all, it was his invention! Even at the very beginning of the nickelodeon era, clergymen and reformers loudly denounced motion pictures for corrupting society's values; films showing crime or juvenile deliquency were held to be exceedingly dangerous influences on the movie-going population, particularly since so many spectators were chil-

Horace G. Plimpton (*left*), Harry Furniss, and Ashley Miller (*right*) discuss a project at the Edison Studio, 1912.

ACTORS, CAMERAMEN, AND TECHNI-
CIANS GATHER AT THE BRONX STUDIO
FOR A HOLIDAY PHOTOGRAPH IN
1911. FOUR DIRECTORS SIT IN FRONT
(ASHLEY MILLER ON LEFT, J. SEARLE
DAWLEY WITH CIGAR).

COVER OF *THE EDISON KINETOGRAM*, VOL. 2, NO. 4, FEATURING *Frankenstein*. THE FILM, RELEASED MARCH 18, 1910, IS DESCRIBED AS "A LIBERAL ADAPTATION OF MRS. SHELLY'S (SIC) FAMOUS STORY....OMIT[TING] ANYTHING WHICH MIGHT BY ANY POSSIBILITY SHOCK ANY PORTION OF AN AUDIENCE."

* In response, the uncredited directors began to run advertisements in the New York *Dramatic Mirror* indicating the films they directed.

dren. Filmmakers were caught on the horns of a dilemma. Sex and violence sold tickets but provoked the outrage of influential citizens. As protests mounted in 1907-08, some cities instituted a policy of censorship, which threatened to disrupt the industry.

Edison was particularly sensitive to the outcry against films. His phonograph appealed to a rural, somewhat prudish clientele while his Portland cement houses and other goods were promoted as family-oriented. It was important not to alienate the public with inappropriate pictures. Finally, Edison's executives did not themselves fully approve of low culture. They believed that motion pictures should do more than amuse the working class; the cinema should uplift and educate.

The Edison company sought to establish the respectability of its pictures in several ways. Prestigious actors, such as Cecil Spooner and Mlle. Pilar Morin, were hired to appear in special films. The company's trade publication, *The Kinetogram*, highlighted the careers of Edison actors, emphasizing their associations with respected theatrical stars. Plimpton also purchased the motion picture rights to well-known literary works, beginning with Mark Twain's *The Prince and the Pauper* (June 1909). By early 1910, *The Kinetogram* featured films based on stories by Bret Harte, Rex Beach, and Richard Harding Davis—well-known writers specializing in tales of the American West. Even here potential controversy was avoided. Bret Harte's *The Luck of Roaring Camp*, which concludes with the death of a child, was given a happy ending; as the film ends "every promise is given for his future welfare." Films were cheerful and optimistic. By 1911 the Edison company advertised the name of the writer for most of its films, suggesting a parallel to respectable literature.*

The Kinetograph Department periodically made films with public service organizations and promoted them heavily. These included *The Man Who Learned* (September 1910), made in cooperation with the New York Milk Committee, and *The Red Cross Seal* (December 1910), with the National Association for the Study and Prevention of Tuberculosis and the American Red Cross. In the former, an old-fashioned farmer milks his cows the traditional way. When his grandchild in the city drinks the milk, the baby almost dies. The farmer learns his lesson the hard way and henceforth takes steps to ensure the safety of his milk. Another series of films focused on American history, including *The Minute Man* (July 1911), *The Capture of Fort Ticonderoga* (July 1911) and *The Declaration of Independence* (August 1911).

Edison films had improved substantially by 1910-11; acting styles became increasingly natural and stories were told clearly. Nothing indicates this improvement better than *The Passerby* (June 1912). Within its flashback structure, an elderly man recalls his life and the crucial moments when he encountered the woman he loved but could never marry. These flashbacks are framed with camera moves toward and away from the speaker's face. As quality improved at Edison, so did the rate of production. Output increased to three reels per week in 1910, four per week in 1911, and five reels commencing in September 1912.

Like other production companies, Edison frequently sent out small groups of actors and production personnel to make films in distant spots. In January 1910, Plimpton dispatched a crew to Cuba where Dawley directed Laura Sawyer in several love stories. Since cold weather and a crowded studio hampered efficient work and novel

THE MAN WHO LEARNED, 1910, PROMOTED PASTEURIZATION OF MILK AND WAS MADE IN COOPERATION WITH THE NEW YORK MILK COMMITTEE. THE FILM WAS ANNOUNCED IN THE EDISON TRADE PUBLICATION THE KINETOGRAM (1910).

scenery boosted interest in the Edison pictures, the additional expense seemed justified. Later that year Dawley traveled to the Rocky Mountains in Canada. In 1911 and 1912, he returned to both locales. Director Ashley Miller took several Edison stars to London. These trips were made in lieu of building a studio on the West Coast (i.e., Hollywood), something that many production companies were doing by 1911.

Edison continued to enjoy handsome profits from filmmaking, ranging from $200,000 to $230,000 per year between 1908 and 1911. In early 1911, Thomas Edison reorganized his commercial activities, combining various business ventures, including his motion pictures, into Thomas A. Edison, Inc. During that year, Edison's domestic sales averaged 40 prints for each

of the 178 pictures released. Foreign sales had been small and of little interest before 1908-09, but by 1911 this had changed dramatically. The Edison company now made two negatives of each subject and shipped one overseas.

Because British exchanges only bought films on an individual basis (rather than placing a standing order for many weeks as in the United States), sales could fluctuate from 100 prints to under 10 for the uniquely American subjects. The impact was noticeable. Edison abandoned American history and concentrated instead on European events. *The Charge of the Light Brigade* (1912), shot by Dawley in Colorado, used American soldiers but costumes reputed to have been shipped from

SCENE FROM *The Charge of the Light Brigade*, 1912. THE ENGLISH PRAISED THIS LAVISH COSTUME SPECTACLE.

England. True or not, the English praised this spectacle and placed an unprecedented print order. Edison executives considered the British market when hiring cartoonist Harry Furniss or purchasing rights to stories. Sales in Australia, South Africa, and South America also assumed more importance to the company.

Between 1906 and 1911, Edison films had not exceeded 1,000 feet in length (eighteen minutes). In the fall of 1911, however, Edison made a few multi-reel subjects which anticipated the longer, feature-length films that would soon dominate the industry. In 1912, this interest shifted and the company introduced the first "serial," *What Happened to Jane*. Each 15-minute film was "complete in itself" but the star (Mary Fuller) and a larger narrative bound the episodes together. The series was prepared in conjunction with *The Ladies' World* magazine which published installments of Jane's adventures corresponding to the films. This tie-in proved extremely popular and Edison was advertising five different series by the beginning of 1914. Although Edison executives decided the serial craze had faded the following year, the serial would remain a staple of motion picture entertainment.

CHAPTER 7
The End of Edison's Movie Career
1912–1918

Edison's motion picture business had achieved stability by the early 1910. The future looked bright, but a series of setbacks ultimately led to the inventor's withdrawal from film production and equipment manufacture. Edison subsidized several aspiring inventors who claimed to be close to solving the problem of producing color films. They never succeeded but two products closer to the inventor's concerns reached fruition. Both the Home Projecting Kinetoscope, which sought to make moving pictures a source of home entertainment, and the updated "Kinetophone," which projected motion pictures with synchronous recorded sound in large theaters, recalled Edison's first caveats. Each, unfortunately, had a devastating effect on his motion picture enterprise.

The Home P.K., as it was called, was designed for use in churches and noncommercial venues as well as homes. It used a 21mm film strip which contained three 5.7mm images across its width; thus each foot of film contained 210 frames. Seventy-seven feet of film ran for 15 minutes. (This compactness recalls the minuscule images generated by Dickson's cylinder experiments over twenty years before.) People could buy the machine and a few films which they could exchange for new films at a small cost. The Home P.K. was launched in late 1911 and was sold primarily by Edison's phonograph dealers.

PROMOTIONAL PHOTOGRAPH OF THE EDISON HOME PROJECTING KINETOSCOPE, CA. 1912. THE HOME P.K. WAS MARKETED "FOR EDUCATION AND ENTERTAINMENT AT HOME, IN SCHOOLS, SUNDAY SCHOOLS, CLUBS, LODGES, ETC."

Films were taken from the catalog of outdated Edison subjects—with some acquisitions made from other members of the Motion Picture Patents Company. Edison employees also made science and educational subjects specifically for the Home P.K. The new motion picture system was difficult to operate and plagued by technical deficiencies. Although Edison and his company invested much money and energy in the Home P.K., it never became very popular or commercially successful.

The Kinetophone, in contrast to the Home P.K., enjoyed initial success. The North American rights were sold to a company set up by prominent vaudeville organizations. The vaudeville theaters embraced the Kinetophone because it differentiated their pictures from those being shown in regular movie houses. They eagerly made an initial three- to six-month commitment to the machine with Edison receiving a rental that varied from $150 to $200 per week. The Kinetophone was applauded by critics when it first appeared on February 19, 1913. With more than fifty machines soon at work, gross income exceeded $10,000 a

week. In addition, as many as a dozen companies toured the country, presenting the novelty in small-town theaters for a few days at a time.

The Kinetophone business boomed into the summer of 1913, but audiences then lost interest. Each reel of film was only six minutes long and pictures usually depicted mediocre vaudeville acts or scenes from plays. As one of Edison's associates fumed, "The public is interested in seeing Talking Pictures as a novelty, once or twice, and then they want longer subjects and first class acting." Although American interest in the Kinetophone novelty was seriously fading by the fall, Edison had sold Kinetophone rights to various organizations overseas, including Japan. These organizations remained viable into 1914; in many instances, only the onset of World War I closed these markets completely.

THE EDISON KINETOPHONE, 1913, COMBINED IMAGES AND SOUND BY SYNCHRONIZING A PROJECTOR WITH A PHONOGRAPH, A DREAM OF EDISON'S SINCE HIS FIRST EXPERIMENTS WITH FILM. THE PUBLIC FLOCKED TO SEE THE NEW WONDER, BUT AFTER SATISFYING THEIR CURIOSITY THEY TURNED AWAY FROM THE SHORT, SIX-MINUTE FILMS THAT FEATURED MEDIOCRE VAUDEVILLE ACTS.

A COMPANY PUBLICITY SHOT SHOWING THE HOME PROJECTING KINETOSCOPE, CA. 1912, DESIGNED TO BRING MOTION PICTURES INTO THE HOME. SO EASY, EVEN A CHILD COULD OPERATE IT.

With all the technical energy put into the Home P.K. and the Kinetophone, Edison failed to keep his regular 35mm projector up-to-date. In 1909 and 1910, profits from the projecting kinetoscope averaged a still respectable $135,000 per year, but down from approximately $200,000. Sales fell 30% in 1911 and were declining rapidly by 1912. Within another two years, this once profitable part of Edison's business had all but ceased to exist. A half-hearted revival was attempted with the development of the "Super-Kinetoscope," in 1915; but it was expensive to manufacture and too high-priced. This attempted revival was soon dropped and with it all efforts to produce motion picture equipment.

Another blow to Edison's motion picture business in mid-decade involved the Motion Picture Patents Company. The Trust had sued almost all unlicensed domestic film producers between 1909 and 1911. While the Patents Company enjoyed initial success against these independents in the courts, Carl Laemmle in particular challenged the validity of its patents and eventually won. Meanwhile the Trust started its own film exchange in mid-1910. The Trust-sponsored General Film Company bought out many of the licensed exchanges; and when a renter refused to sell, he soon discovered that his Patents Company license had been cancelled. Tactics such as these led the United States government to bring an antitrust suit on August 15, 1912. Damaging evidence was amassed, and on October 1, 1915, the courts found the Motion Picture Patents Company guilty. Edison and other licensed producers then became liable for triple damages to injured parties. This defeat was not only a costly commercial setback but a public relations disaster.

The antitrust case preoccupied Edison and his allies while a significant change was overtaking the motion picture industry—the advent of feature-length (one hour or longer) films; the company's failure to make a timely transition to feature filmmaking proved devastating. Edison released only one-reelers throughout 1912 and most of 1913, even as the average number of prints sold per subject fell from forty to about thirty. That August, Edison introduced one two-reeler per week. Sales quickly picked up, halving the previous drop-off. Feature films (and even two-reelers were considered features at this stage) were in great demand while one-reelers were becoming "filler." Nonetheless, the Edison company regularly released four one-reelers and one two-reeler each week through the beginning of 1915. Outside its regular release schedule, the company made only a few tentative experiments—such as *My Friend from India* (August 1914), a special, 3 1/2-reel feature distributed by the General Film Company. The film cost a modest $5,548 to make; yet a year later it had still not turned a profit. In mid-1914 Edison began to release one three-reel subject a month, but such "features" did not become a regular part of Edison's weekly output until March 1915. By then *The Birth of a Nation* had opened and Paramount had been regularly releasing pictures of four to six reels for a year and a half. By the end of 1915 Edison had ceased to make one-reelers for regular release because the undertaking had become a money-losing proposition.

William Hodkinson, president of Paramount Pictures Corporation, had come to rely on block booking (in which a theater contracted for all its programs for a full year) and arrangements whereby his company received a percentage of the gross receipts. These commercial strategies ensured healthy profits for Famous Players Film Company and Jesse Lasky Feature Film Company, which were producing the films. The General Film Company's failure to pursue such innovative methods made feature film production unprofitable for Edison. Finally, in mid-1915, Edison began using outside distributors for its features, including Paramount and George Kleine. Profits, it was assumed, would be substantial. The Kleine-Edison Feature Service was inaugurated with the release of *Vanity Fair* in October 1915. Although it starred Minnie Maddern Fiske, the renowned stage actress, income was disappointing and the picture may have never recovered its cost of $28,676.

The advent of features and World War I (which curtailed foreign markets) destroyed Edison's profits. The Motion Picture Division barely broke even during 1915 and 1916. To compensate for the decline in revenues, Edison brought in an efficiency engineer, S. B. Mambert, who was determined to keep expenses down. When filmmaking costs rose substantially in mid-1915, Horace Plimpton was fired. L. W. McChesney became head of the Motion Picture Division that August. Bureaucratization and petty paperwork proliferated in an attempt to reduce waste. The impact, other than further disruption, was small; filmmaking costs failed to go down. Directors were ordered to work with exceedingly low (4 to 3) shooting ratios,* which inevitably hampered production and harmed quality. The cost of a film was more important to Edison executives than its potential box-office success.

Since the second half of 1915, the Edison

NOTICE
GREATEST SENSATION OF THE CENTURY
"THE EDISON KINETOPHONE"
LAUGHING ♦ SINGING ♦ TALKING ♦ PICTURES

BROADSIDE FOR 1913-1914 KINETOPHONE TOUR IN CHILE (MISSPELLED CHILI), ADVERTISING A PROGRAM CONSISTING OF "OPERA, MUSICAL COMEDY, VAUDEVILLE, MINSTREL, ETC. BOTH IN SPANISH AND ENGLISH."

* Shooting ratio refers to the ratio of film shot to film used. Today, a low shooting ratio would be 15 to 1: for every fifteen feet of film that is shot, one foot is used. A 4 to 3 shooting ratio seems almost incomprehensible. It essentially meant that everything was shot only once and there was no room for experimentation.

company had released its films through a variety of organizations. This diluted their identity as Edison productions and often created minor conflicts between exhibitors who found their exclusives undermined. The Paramount deal, which had looked highly promising in 1915, progressed slowly and then soured after the company acquired only three Edison features. Beginning in October 1916, the Kleine-Edison Feature Service was expanded to include former members of the Motion Picture Patents Company. The new K. E. S. E. Service involved Kleine, Edison, Selig, and Essanay. Edison also made films for McClure Pictures during 1916.

Regardless of distributor, Edison pictures appealed to moralistic middle-class reform groups, an appeal that only intensified when America entered World War I in April 1917. As influential organizations called for moral purity in films, Edison inaugurated a series known as "Conquest Pictures." These programs were meant to provide "cleaner and more wholesome films, which could be exhibited with safety before any member of the family." The unexciting results were poorly received and financially disappointing. By the beginning of 1918 Edison was eager to leave the filmmaking business. In February, thirty years after meeting Eadweard Muybridge, the inventor laid off his actors and production staff. On March 30, 1918, Thomas A. Edison, Inc. sold its studio and plant to the Lincoln & Parker Film Company for $150,000 cash and $200,000 in common and preferred stock. Edison's role in filmmaking had come to an end.

Having finally abandoned filmmaking, Edison became a figure revered by all sectors of the motion picture industry. By the 1920s he had mastered the role of the benevolent sage. In 1929 he became the first honorary member of the

Academy of Motion Picture Arts and Sciences. Within a decade of his death, a Hollywood company (Metro-Goldwyn-Mayer) that had once been the inventor's competitor made two biographical portraits of Edison: *Young Tom Edison* starring Mickey Rooney and *Edison the Man* with Spencer Tracy. It was not until the 1960s and 1970s that historians looked behind the celebratory biographies and found a more complex figure. Rejecting the myths, they were often angry that the idealized portrait had not been real. As a result Edison came under severe critical attack. Historians such as Gordon Hendricks accused Edison of being a bully, a miser, a liar, an ingrate—even a thief who had stolen credit for the invention of motion pictures from W.K.L. Dickson.

As we celebrate the 100th anniversary of motion pictures, it is our task to seek a balance between mythmaking and simple debunking. Today's motion pictures are direct descendants of those shown in Edison's first peep-hole kinetoscopes. If the "Wizard of Menlo

Vanity Fair, 1915, one of Edison's early feature-length films, starred the noted stage actress Minnie Maddern Fiske.

Park" had not moved to West Orange and invented an instrument which does for the eye what the phonograph does for the ear, we would still have motion pictures. But they probably would have been an English or French invention—not an American one. The beginnings of motion pictures would have occurred later and the technology been somewhat different. Rather than embracing America's vibrant popular culture, the first movies might have been more elitist and genteel.

But it was Edison who gathered together and synthesized the key ideas that made possible the invention of motion pictures. He supplied the laboratory, the financing, the impetus, and the right personnel to help realize his vision. His filmmaking company went on to make over 4,000 pictures in the twenty-five years between 1893 and 1918. Incredibly, most of these films survive. These contributions, along with his invention, development, and commercial exploitation of the phonograph make Thomas Edison the progenitor of today's technology-based entertainment industry. Obviously, he depended on the help of collaborators and employees. Perhaps almost as obviously, his career as a businessman did not live up to the standards we sometimes expect of our heroes. Having absorbed the shock of Edison's humanity, however, we may finally be able to judge his achievements on their own terms. Perhaps more than any other single individual, he propelled America and the world into the twentieth century.

EDISON'S FUNERAL, OCTOBER 1931. NEWSREEL CAMERAS RECORD THE THOUSANDS OF MOURNERS AS THEY ENTER THE MAIN LABORATORY WHERE EDISON'S BODY LAY IN STATE. MOTION PICTURES, SO MUCH AN EDISON INVENTION, ARE PRESENT AT HIS FAREWELL.

The End

❧ An Edison Chronology ❧

1847
FEBRUARY 11: BORN IN MILAN, OHIO

1859-1863
WORKS AS A NEWSBOY AND "CANDY BUTCH-ER" ON THE GRAND TRUNK RAILROAD

1863
SPRING: BECOMES A TELEGRAPH OPERATOR IN PORT HURON, MICHIGAN

1863-1868
WORKS AS AN ITINERANT TELEGRAPH OPERATOR; CONDUCTS TELEGRAPH EXPERIMENTS

1869
JANUARY 30: RESIGNS FROM WESTERN UNION AND DEVOTES HIMSELF FULL-TIME TO INVENTING AND PURSUING VARIOUS TELEGRAPH ENTERPRISES

1871
DECEMBER 25: MARRIES MARY STILLWELL

1874
SPRING-SUMMER: INVENTS THE QUADRUPLEX TELEGRAPH THAT CAN SEND FOUR MESSAGES OVER THE SAME WIRE SIMULTANEOUSLY

1875
SPRING-SUMMER: DEVELOPS "ELECTRIC PEN" FOR MAKING MULTIPLE COPIES OF A LETTER

1876
MARCH: MOVES EXPERIMENTAL LABOR-ATORY TO MENLO PARK, NEW JERSEY

1877
FALL: DEVELOPS CARBON BUTTON TELE-PHONE TRANSMITTER

1877
DECEMBER 7: EXHIBITS TIN-FOIL PHONO-GRAPH AT THE OFFICES OF *SCIENTIFIC AMERICAN*, NEW YORK CITY

1879
DECEMBER 31: HOLDS FIRST DEMON-STRATION OF HIS INCANDESCENT ELECTRIC LIGHTING SYSTEM AT MENLO PARK LABORATORY

1882
SEPTEMBER 4: OPENS PEARL STREET CEN-TRAL STATION IN LOWER MANHATTAN--THE FIRST PERMANENT COMMERCIAL ELECTRIC POWER GENERATING STATION

1884
AUGUST 9: WIFE, MARY, DIES

1886
FEBRUARY 24: MARRIES MINA MILLER

SPRING: MOVES TO GLENMONT, HIS NEW HOME IN LLEWELLYN PARK, WEST ORANGE, NEW JERSEY

1887
DECEMBER: OPENS HIS WEST ORANGE LABORATORY

1888
FEBRUARY 27: EADWARD MUYBRIDGE VISITS EDISON AT HIS LABORATORY; PROPOS-ES COMBINING HIS ZOOPRAXISCOPE WITH EDISON'S PHONOGRAPH

JUNE: EDISON AND OTHER EXPERIMENTERS DEVELOP THE "PERFECTED" PHONOGRAPH

OCTOBER 8: WRITES FIRST MOTION PIC-TURE CAVEAT

1889
JUNE: W.K.L. DICKSON FORMALLY ASSIGNED TO EDISON'S MOTION PICTURE PROJECT AS CHIEF EXPERIMENTER

1891
MAY 20: SHOWS EXPERIMENTAL 3/4" MOTION PICTURES TO MEMBERS OF FEDERA-TION OF WOMEN'S CLUBS AT HIS WEST ORANGE LABORATORY

1892
OCTOBER: FRAMES OF EDISON'S 1 1/2" (APPROXIMATELY 35MM) MOTION PICTURES FIRST PUBLISHED IN *THE PHONOGRAM*

1893
FEBRUARY: BLACK MARIA MOTION PIC-TURE STUDIO COMPLETED AT THE EDISON LABORATORY, WEST ORANGE

MAY 9: EDISON'S 1 1/2" (35 MM) MOTION PICTURES FIRST SHOWN AT BROOKLYN INSTITUTE OF ARTS AND SCIENCES

1894
APRIL 1: MOTION PICTURE PROJECT SHIFTED FROM LABORATORY ACCOUNTS TO THE EDISON MANUFACTURING COMPANY

APRIL 14: FIRST KINETOSCOPE PARLOR OPENS AT 1155 BROADWAY, NEW YORK CITY

1896
APRIL 23: "EDISON'S VITASCOPE" PREMIERES AT KOSTER & BIAL'S MUSIC HALL, NEW YORK CITY

1897
AUGUST 31: EDISON RECEIVES PATENT FOR MOTION PICTURE CAMERA

1901
FEBRUARY: EDISON MOTION PICTURE STUDIO AT 41 EAST TWENTY-FIRST STREET GOES INTO OPERATION

1903
DECEMBER: *THE GREAT TRAIN ROBBERY* PREMIERES

1907
JULY 15: EDISON'S MOTION PICTURE STU-DIO IN THE BRONX GOES INTO OPERATION

1908
DECEMBER 18: MOTION PICTURE PATENTS COMPANY FORMED

1909
FALL: MARKETS SUCCESSFUL STORAGE BATTERY

1911
FEBRUARY 28: ORGANIZES THOMAS A. EDISON, INC.

1915
FALL: HEADS NEWLY FORMED NAVAL CONSULTING BOARD

1918
MARCH 30 : SELLS BRONX STUDIO AND MOTION PICTURE INTERESTS

1929
OCTOBER 21: IS HONORED AT LIGHT'S GOLDEN JUBILEE

1931
OCTOBER 18: DIES AT GLENMONT

❧ Picture Credits ❧

Title page: U.S. Department of the Interior, National Park Service, Edison National Historic Site, West Orange, New Jersey

Copyright page: International Museum of Photography, George Eastman House, Rochester, New York

p. viii: U.S. Department of the Interior, National Park Service, Edison National Historic Site, West Orange, New Jersey

p. 2: U.S. Department of the Interior, National Park Service, Edison National Historic Site, West Orange, New Jersey

p. 4: U.S. Department of the Interior, National Park Service, Edison National Historic Site, West Orange, New Jersey

p. 5: Courtesy of the Stanford University Museum of Art, Stanford, California

pp. 6-7: U.S. Department of the Interior, National Park Service, Edison National Historic Site, West Orange, New Jersey

p. 7: U.S. Department of the Interior, National Park Service, Edison National Historic Site, West Orange, New Jersey

p. 8: Gordon Hendricks Collection, Smithsonian Institution, Washington, D.C.

p. 9, center and right: U.S. Department of the Interior, National Park Service, Edison National Historic Site, West Orange, New Jersey

p. 10 left: U.S. Department of the Interior, National Park Service, Edison National Historic Site, West Orange, New Jersey

p. 10 center: U.S. Department of the Interior, National Park Service, Edison National Historic Site, West Orange, New Jersey

p.11: U.S. Department of the Interior, National Park Service, Edison National Historic Site, West Orange, New Jersey

pp. 12-13: U.S. Department of the Interior, National Park Service, Edison National Historic Site, East Orange, New Jersey

pp. 14-15: Museum of Modern Art/Film Stills Archive, New York

p. 15: Smithsonian Institution, Washington, D.C.

p. 16: U.S. Department of the Interior, National Park Service, Edison National Historic Site, West Orange, New Jersey

p. 17: Ray Phillips Collection

p. 18: U.S. Department of the Interior, National Park Service, Edison National Historic Site, West Orange, New Jersey

p. 19 center: Museum of Modern Art/Film Stills Archive, New York

p. 19 right: U.S. Department of the Interior, National Park Service, Edison National Historic Site, West Orange, New Jersey

p. 20: U.S. Department of the Interior, National Park Service, Edison National Historic Site, West Orange, New Jersey

pp. 20-21: U.S. Department of the Interior, National Park Service, Edison National Historic Site

p. 22 left: Museum of Modern Art/Film Stills Archive, New York

p. 22 center: U.S. Department of the Interior, National Park Service, Edison National Historic Site, West Orange, New Jersey

p. 23: National Archives and Records Administration

pp. 24-25: Museum of Modern Art/Film Stills Archive, New York

p. 25: National Archives and Records Administration

p. 26: Museum of Modern Art/Film Stills Archive, New York

p. 27 top: Museum of Modern Art/Film Stills Archive, New York

p. 27 bottom: U.S. Department of the Interior, National Park Service, Edison National Historic Site, West Orange, New Jersey

p. 28: Library of Congress, Motion Picture, Broadcasting, and Recorded Sound Division, Washington, D.C.

❧ PICTURE CREDITS ❧

p. 29: U.S. Department of the Interior, National Park Service, Edison National Historic Site, West Orange, New Jersey

p. 30 top: Library of Congress, Motion Picture, Broadcasting, and Recorded Sound Division, Washington, D.C.

p. 30 bottom: National Archives and Records Administration, College Park, Maryland

p. 31: U.S. Department of the Interior, National Park Service, Edison National Historic Site, West Orange, New Jersey

p. 32: Library of Congress, Motion Picture, Broadcasting, and Recorded Sound Division, Washington, D.C.

p. 33: Library of Congress, Motion Picture, Broadcasting, and Recorded Sound Division, Washington, D.C.

p. 34: U.S. Department of the Interior, National Park Service, Edison National Historic Site, West Orange, New Jersey

p. 35: Film Department, International Museum of Photography, George Eastman House, Rochester, New York

pp. 36-37: U.S. Department of the Interior, National Park Service, Edison National Historic Site, West Orange, New Jersey

p. 37: U.S. Department of the Interior, National Park Service, Edison National Historic Site, West Orange, New Jersey

p. 38: Film Department, International Museum of Photography, George Eastman House, Rochester, New York

p. 39: Museum of Modern Art/Film Stills Archive, New York

p. 40: U.S. Department of the Interior, National Park Service, Edison National Historic Site, West Orange, New Jersey

p. 41: U.S. Department of the Interior, National Park Service, Edison National Historic Site, West Orange, New Jersey

p. 42: U.S. Department of the Interior, National Park Service, Edison National Historic Site, West Orange, New Jersey

p. 44: U.S. Department of the Interior, National Park Service, Edison National Historic Site, West Orange, New Jersey

p. 45: U.S. Department of the Interior, National Park Service, Edison National Historic Site, West Orange, New Jersey

p. 46: U.S. Department of the Interior, National Park Service, Edison National Historic Site, West Orange, New Jersey

p. 47: U.S. Department of the Interior, National Park Service, Edison National Historic Site, West Orange, New Jersey

p. 48: U.S. Department of the Interior, National Park Service, Edison National Historic Site, West Orange, New Jersey

p. 49: U.S. Department of the Interior, National Park Service, Edison National Historic Site, West Orange, New Jersey

p. 50: U.S. Department of the Interior, National Park Service, Edison National Historic Site, West Orange, New Jersey

p. 51: U.S. Department of the Interior, National Park Service, Edison National Historic Site, West Orange, New Jersey

p. 52: U.S. Department of the Interior, National Park Service, Edison National Historic Site, West Orange, New Jersey

pp. 52-53: U.S. Department of the Interior, National Park Service, Edison National Historic Site, West Orange, New Jersey

p. 54: U.S. Department of the Interior, National Park Service, Edison National Historic Site, West Orange, New Jersey

p. 55: Museum of Modern Art/Film Stills Archive, New York

p. 56: U.S. Department of the Interior, National Park Service, Edison National Historic Site, West Orange, New Jersey

❧ BIBLIOGRAPHY ❧

This overview of Edison's engagement with motion pictures is based on two book-length treatments by the author: *The Emergence of Cinema: The American Screen to 1907* (New York: Scribner's, 1990) and *Before the Nickelodeon: Edwin S. Porter and the Edison Manufacturing Company* (Berkeley: University of California Press, 1991). Both studies include extensive footnotes and can be consulted by the reader interested in sources and additional information. The earlier book also has an extensive bibliography. A substantial publication industry has grown up around Thomas Edison and his various inventions. The work currently being done by the staff of the Thomas A. Edison Papers will ultimately require a major revision of the historical record. Preclassical (pre-1918) cinema has also been extensively investigated in recent years. The bibliography that follows is therefore highly selective.

Eileen Bowser, *The Transformation of Cinema: 1907-1915*. New York: Scribner's, 1990.

Noel Burch, *Life to Those Shadows: Contributions to the History of Film Language, 1902-1914*. Berkeley: University of California Press, 1991.

Thomas Elsaesser with Adam Barker, eds., *Early Cinema: Space, Frame, Narrative*. London: British Film Institute, 1990.

John Fell, *Film and the Narrative Tradition*. Norman: University of Oklahoma Press, 1974. Reprint, Berkeley: University of California Press.

------.ed., *Film Before Griffith*. Berkeley: University of California Press, 1983.

Robert Friedel, Paul Israel, with Bernard S. Finn, *Edison's Electric Light: Biography of an Invention*. New Brunswick, N.J.: Rutgers University Press, 1986.

Tom Gunning, *D. W. Griffith and the Rise of the Narrative Film*. Urbana: University of Illinois Press, 1991.

Gordon Hendricks, *The Edison Motion Picture Myth*. Berkeley: University of California Press, 1961. Reprint, New York: Arno, 1972.

------. *The Kinetoscope: America's First Commercially Successful Motion Picture Exhibitor*. 1966. Reprint, New York: Arno, 1972.

Thomas Parke Hughes, *Thomas Edison, Professional Inventor*. London: HMSO, 1976.

------. *Networks of Power: Electrification in Western Society, 1880-1930*. Baltimore: Johns Hopkins University Press, 1983.

Reese V. Jenkins, *Images and Enterprise: Technology and the American Photographic Industry, 1839-1925*. Baltimore: Johns Hopkins University Press, 1975.

------. and others, ed., *The Papers of Thomas A. Edison, Vol. 1: The Making of an Inventor (February 1847-June 1873)*. Baltimore: Johns Hopkins University Press, 1989.

Matthew Josephson, *Edison*. New York: McGraw-Hill, 1959.

Andre Millard, *Edison and the Business of Innovation*. Baltimore: Johns Hopkins University Press, 1990.

Robert A. Rosenberg, Paul B. Israel, Keith A. Nier, Melodie Andrews, *The Papers of Thomas A. Edison, Vol. 2: From Workshop to Laboratory (June 1873-March 1876)*. Baltimore: Johns Hopkins University Press, 1991.

Ben Singer, "Early Home Cinema and the Edison Home Projecting Kinetoscope." *Film History* 2 (1988), 37-69.

Robert Sklar, *Movie-Made America: A Cultural History of American Movies*. New York: Random House, 1975.

Paul C. Spehr, *The Movies Begin: Making Movies in New Jersey, 1887-1920*. Newark, N.J.: Newark Museum, 1977.

CHARLES MUSSER
IS ASSISTANT PROFESSOR
OF FILM STUDIES AND AMERICAN
STUDIES AT YALE
UNIVERSITY. THIS PUBLICATION
DRAWS ON HIS THREE CRITICALLY
ACCLAIMED BOOKS,
*THE EMERGENCE OF CINEMA:
THE AMERICAN SCREEN TO 1907*
(SCRIBNER'S);
*BEFORE THE NICKELODEON:
EDWIN S. PORTER AND
THE EDISON MANUFACTURING
COMPANY* (UNIVERSTITY OF
CALIFORNIA PRESS);
AND, WITH CAROL NELSON, *HIGH-
CLASS MOVING PICTURES:
LYMAN H. HOWE AND THE
FORGOTTEN ERA OF TRAVELING
EXHIBITION, 1880-1920*
(PRINCETON UNIVERSITY PRESS).
HE ALSO SERVED AS
CATALOG EDITOR FOR *A GUIDE TO
MOTION PICTURE CATALOGS* BY
AMERICAN PRODUCERS
AND DISTRIBUTORS, 1984-1908:
A MICROFIM EDITION, PUBLISHED
AS PART OF THE
THOMAS A. EDISON PAPERS
HISTORICAL EDITING PROJECT.

JACKET DESIGN BY NINA OVRYN

ON THE COVER:
SEVERAL PRODUCTIONS
UNDERWAY SIMULTANEOUSLY AT
THE BRONX STUDIO,
CA. 1913. SINCE THE FILMS WERE
SILENT, THE NOISES OF
THE ADJACENT SETS OR OF NEARBY
CONSTRUCTION DID
NOT INTERFERE WITH FILMING.

 Colophon

This book was designed and composed on the Macintosh IIci, with the software program Quark Xpress 3.1. The text of the book is set in Adobe Goudy Roman, with italics. The typeface was originally designed by Frederic W. Goudy for American Typefounders in 1915-1916.

The large drop caps that are found at the beginning of each chapter, and used throughout the text are set in Charlemagne.

The typefaces used in the chapter headings are Copperplate Gothic, also designed by F.W. Goudy, and Bordeux.

This book was printed and bound in the United States by Bookcrafters, Inc., Chelsea, Michigan.

It is printed on 60-pound Patina Matte.